Praise for the Book

"'Hi Mom, It's Me,' by Nancy Yuskaitis, offers rich encouragement for those who are grieving, especially those who are grieving the death of loved ones. It can be a vital source of hope in the midst of unspeakable heartbreak. In relating her personal journey around the deaths of her daughters, Lavender and Crystal (the Soulful Starlights), Yuskaitis describes the power of miracles and also practical steps that can bring relief and greater life balance in the face of profound loss. She emphasizes the importance of self-love, self-care, and not grieving alone, three elements I believe are key in learning how to reframe grief. This book can be a gentle and instructive companion for readers who may be seeking friendship as they find their way with grief and knowing they are not alone."

—**Ellen Antill, M.A., Grief Counselor**

"Nancy has given those who grieve an amazing gift, which reminds us that death does not affect the bonds of love we share with our departed child, and our unconditional love can bring us connectedness and peace even though we've gone through the worst nightmare any parent could have. This is an intimate, courageous work offering a look into the universals in the healing journey from learning to navigate devastating grief to a sense of oneness with life and an expanded sense of love for all that is. She offers many different ways to cooperate with our healing process, including art therapy, music, and 'Soulful suggestions.' Her quotes at the end give much food for 'Soul thoughts.' Those who enter this healing journey will be transformed in beautiful ways by the time they finish this book."

—**Robert Wilkinson, Author of *Love Dad:***
Healing the Grief of Losing a Stillborn

"'Hi, Mom, It's Me: Hope, Love, and the Afterlife' is a beam of light, lighting the path out of despair onto the journey of hope for the weary. Written from the depth of her heart and from the intention to be of service, Nancy Yuskaitis reveals her personal journey from inconsolable grief and loss to the discovery that relationships do exist after death and that love never dies. The book is authentic and courageous; a road map filled with knowledge and insights; a must-read for anyone in search of answers. It shines a light and illuminates the gifts on the other side of loss."

—**Laurie D. Kerge**

"Gently, step by step the author guides you through her healing journey. As she shares with you with great love, empathy, and compassion her story of how, in her own words: 'I truly feel as if I've experienced a miracle of transforming my devastatingly heavy grief into a softer, lighter, gentler grief through this experience'. Join Nancy as you take the journey of a lifetime, mentored and supported by her loving presence by your side as you too, by the end of the book, realize that such miracles are possible."

—**Jonathon Hope, Spirit Release Practitioner**

"For bereaved parents seeking help to navigate traumatic grief, 'Hi Mom, It's Me: Hope, Love, and the Afterlife' is a precious gem. As a mother who lost two daughters, Nancy takes us on a journey through her losses and the many ways she found comfort through afterlife communication, meditation, mindfulness, spirit guides, and angelic realms. Through detailed accounts of afterlife conversations with her daughters, helpful spiritual practices, and an abundance of journal prompts and guided meditations, Nancy offers a generous set of tools that we can use for our own transformation and healing. This radiant book feels like a compassionate friend and wise companion for the mind, body, and spirit during the darkest seasons of grief. I will use this book as a guide for many years to come, but after one read, it has already changed my life."

—**Mary Davis, Author of *Every Day Spirit***

"There is so much in this book that is of value. The author bravely lays open her raw and honest feelings about the loss of two children but misery memoir, this is not. It is an inspiring, beautiful, and uplifting account. For the grieving, with empathy and realism, the author shares how she transformed her desperately sad feelings into greater connection, peace, and hope. She also offers her insights into various aspects of the Spirit World and how soothing communication with deceased loved ones can be. For those of us just looking for greater well-being in our lives, Nancy reveals the practices that helped her not only through her darkest of times but the ones she uses regularly, even today."

—Naila Hope, Director/Practitioner of Therapies of Hope

"I applaud Nancy Yuskaitis's conviction of courage. A beautifully written, compelling account of grief and loss, Hi Mom, It's Me, takes you from despair and heartache, to blossoming in mindfulness. Nancy empowers the reader with purpose and compassion, encouraging them to be fully present to love and to be loved by those who have passed on—death is not an end, but only a transition. With several tools available throughout the book to guide you while actively participating in your journey, you will reframe fear, resentment, and regret into grace and acceptance, allowing for profound and meaningful relationships with signs from your loved ones in the spirit world, which ultimately leads to healing. We can be deeply touched and uplifted when our loved ones communicate with us in various ways; it confirms we are never apart. Nancy eloquently reminds us to elevate our perspective and actively reframe anxiety, worry, and fear into gratitude, peace, and positive action, so that our experiences reflect the creative genius of our soul."

—Paula M. Robinson, RN, Healthcare Executive, Contributing Author of *Priceless Caregiving: Stories of Elder Care Success, Courage and Strength*

"A mother's tender journey through double grief, Nancy Yuskaitis shows us there is indeed, light at the end of the tunnel."

—Eve Simmons

Hi Mom, It's Me

Hope, Love, and the Afterlife

Nancy Yuskaitis

Global Book Publishing

Hi Mom, It's Me
Nancy Yuskaitis
©2025 Nancy Yuskaitis
All rights reserved.

All rights reserved. No part of this publication may be reproduced, distributed, or transmitted in any form or by any means, including photocopying, recording, or other electronic or mechanical methods, without the prior written permission of the author or publisher (except by a reviewer, who may quote brief passages and/or show brief video clips in a review).

ISBN: 978-1-964644-46-2
Book Design & Publishing done by:
Global Book Publishing
www.globalbookpublishing.com

Disclaimer: The Publisher and the Author make no representations or warranties with respect to the accuracy and completeness of this work and especially disclaim all warranties, including without limitation warranties of fitness for a particular purpose. No warranty may be created or extended by sales or promotional materials. The advice and strategies contained herein may not be suitable for every situation. This work is sold with the understanding that the Publisher is not engaged in rendering legal, accounting, or other professional services. If professional assistance is required, the services of a competent professional person should be sought. Neither the Publisher nor the Author shall be liable for the damages arising here from. The fact that an organization or website is referred to in this work as a citation or potential source of further information does not mean that the Author or the Publisher endorses the information the organization or the website may provide or recommendations it may make. Further, readers should be aware that internet websites listed in this work may have changed or disappeared between when this work was written and when it is used.

DISCLAIMER

This book is intended for educational and informational purposes only. It is not a substitute for professional medical or mental health consultation. The author of this book does not dispense medical advice or prescribe the use of any technique as a form of treatment for physical, emotional, or medical situations. Readers are responsible for their own healthcare decisions and choices based on the information presented in this book. The author and publisher do not accept responsibility for any adverse effects individuals may claim to experience, whether directly or indirectly in relation to the information contained in this book. Individual results may vary, and the author cannot guarantee specific outcomes.

The stories in this book are true accounts taken from my personal life and reading sessions. The names and other identifying characteristics of individuals have been changed to protect anonymity. Any similarities to a known person are coincidental, unintentional, or with permission.

No part of this book may be reproduced or transmitted in any form, or by any means, electronic or mechanical, including photography, recording, or in any information storage or retrieval system without the written permission from the author or publisher, except by a reviewer, who may quote brief passages embodied in articles and reviews.

This book is dedicated to my family in both realms, including my daughters, Crystal and Lavender, who provide confirmation that love and life continue on in adventures of soulful inspired living.

Table of Contents

Letter to the Reader   *xiii*

Introduction   *xv*

Section 1: Love Is Alive   19

   1. Between Two Worlds   22
   2. Hope Brightens the Darkest Days   25
   3. Into the Light   30
   4. Gone without Goodbye   32
   5. The First Hello   37
   6. Waking Up on the Other Side   44

Section 2: Meet the Soulful Starlights   49

   7. Soulful Starlight Sessions   52
   8. Life in Another Realm   55
   9. A Life Review in Two Worlds   57
   10. You Are Not Alone   61
   11. Angels in Our Midst   68
   12. Support Is Always Available   72
   13. Your Spiritual Guidance Team   79
   14. Jovial Angels, Spirit Guides, & Muses   83

Section 3: Grief Journey   88

   15. Life after Child Loss   91
   16. Soulful Grief Reflections   96
   17. Soulful Self-Love & Self-Care   120
   18. Special Days of Significance   136
   19. Peace, Passion, Mindfulness, & Joy   149

Section 4: Mystical, Magical, Mindful Moments   **158**

  20. Waiting for the Rainbow   161
  21. Spirit Signs and Scenes   169
  22. Meditation & Soulful Intuitive Writing   189

Section 5: The Art of Soulful Inspired Living   **208**

  23. Mystical, Magical, and Mindful   211
  24. Soulful Inspired Adventures   217
  25. Soulful Adventures Challenge   250
  26. Soulful Messages   255

Closing Thoughts   **262**
Acknowledgment   **265**
About the Author   **267**

Letter to the Reader

Soulful greetings, beautiful souls,

As a mother of two children in the afterlife, I genuinely share with you in the following pages, my experiences and the encouragement I received in a transformational journey with my daughters, angels, and spirit guides to uplift and inspire you as you navigate your own grief journey while holding your loved one close to your heart.

At some point in our lives, we are all touched by loss, and in doing so, one may wonder what happens after we leave this life on earth for the world beyond. I certainly longed to know the answer after the sudden loss of my baby daughter all those years ago.

In this book, you will discover the answers I received, as well as much more about life, loss, and the afterlife. I hope you will find comfort, solace, and peace as you embark on this journey with me. Thank you for being here.

This is my story of the unimaginable heartbreak of child loss as well as the remarkable life-changing renewal that occurred in the blending of our two worlds through afterlife conversations with my two daughters.

It is a story filled with the seasons of my grief journey as I discover how to go on living amid shattered dreams. In the following pages, you will read about my experiences of loss as a very young mother with Lavender and again four decades later with Crystal.

This journey unfolded in wondrous ways, beginning with the initial contact and continuing with each of them individually, which offered immense peace, hope, and healing to my broken heart. The messages I will share with you are in collaboration with Lavender and Crystal in spirit, who not only confirmed their safety and aliveness in the afterlife but also prompted the writing of this book to inspire you as you strive to heal from traumatic loss.

I truly understand that your life has completely changed by your loved one's passing, and so have you in carrying the heavy weight of grief, sadness, and pain. In my own grief, I found that we are not meant to carry this burden alone. There are caring souls on earth and in the world beyond who can assist you.

I will share with you how developing a relationship with your angels, spirit guides, and loved ones on the other side is beneficial to your well-being. You will also find the spiritual life coaching I received from spirit to lighten my grief, navigate loss, and embark on a soulful journey, one day at a time.

I invite you to start where you are, honor your feelings, and cultivate a sense of compassion for yourself as you explore new ways to nurture your body, heart, and soul.

Introduction

Hi Mom, It's Me

As a young girl growing up in South Florida, the firstborn of four children, I learned at an early age that family life had its challenges. Yet, I always knew I wanted to get married, have children, and live an island life.

I embarked on this fairy tale with my high school boyfriend while in my senior year of high school. We began our family quickly; our sweet son was born, and within two years, I gave birth to our lovely daughter. I was ecstatic and felt my family was complete.

Sadly, life turned, and in a tragic moment, my dream of a happy family was crushed, and I was in complete despair after the sudden passing of my infant baby girl. In times of tragedy, one never knows how to go about living in a changed reality or whether one will even survive it. It was like that for me; losing a child was never something that even came to my mind as a young mother. In fact, I didn't even know of anyone who had lost a child at that point in time.

I struggled with my grief in a challenging family dynamic as my third child, another daughter, arrived full of promise and joy. Life would change again in divorce, and I worked hard to provide for my two beautiful children, all the while grieving alone.

Decades later, the unthinkable happened again, and my adult daughter suddenly left this world, leaving me sorrowful. Yet I was encouraged to discover ways to survive heartbreak and to live out my life in memory of both of my girls.

I share this with you as a mother who has learned to nurture her broken heart back to soulful resilience and who intends to light the path for others along the way. I will not try to rush your grief process. In fact, there will be times I encourage you to lean into it, to feel it, to acknowledge it, and also to release the trauma associated with it as I have done in self-protection. I realized that time does not heal all. It takes what I call soulful intention as you learn to live with a softer grief by your side.

I appreciate that I am not a therapist or medical provider, but a mother who has been through the devastating loss of two children. In this book, you will discover how I came to connect with my two daughters in the afterlife and the gifts of grace and guidance I received during my darkest times.

My compassion is with you, supporting you with gentle encouragement as I take you on a journey into the lessons I've learned in releasing sorrow, comforting a broken heart, soothing a weary soul, and living with loss.

This book is for anyone seeking a deeper understanding of the afterlife and how afterlife communication can be a truly life-enhancing experience. It is also for those who support the bereaved with an open mind, whether as a grief coach, grief therapist, meditation teacher, mindfulness guide, intuitive medium, energy worker, or support group leader, and I welcome you.

The topics I've included are wide-ranging, including grief recovery, spiritual life coaching, mediumship, soulful living, meditation, Reiki, journaling, and expressive art as self-care modalities. There are questions to ask and prompts to write as you are encouraged to create your own soulful grief journey.

Introduction

I would like to introduce you to my daughters, the Soulful Starlights, who banded together to brighten my world when I had lost my purpose and passion for living in a very heavy and sad reality—one where my husband, son, and our family lived on earth while my daughters lived in heaven. The spirit world responded with an abundance of support, uplifting my life and opening my heart to rediscover meaning and purpose amidst suffering.

In the midst of my emotional pain, change began to occur in the gentlest of ways in the pages of my journal. As I poured my emotions out on paper, I could sense the presence of my loving daughters around me. Each morning, I was called to awaken to write where I would spend quality mother–daughter time being immersed in the loving messages from the Soulful Starlights.

They introduced me to the concept of The Art of Soulful Inspired Living, which helped me navigate my grief and share it with others, as well as Mystical, Magical, Mindful Moments, and Messages, designed to foster healing beyond loss in ways that uplift and inspire creativity and joy.

My experience has shown me that we are all given opportunities to be a light for others in various ways, and this is what I have been given to share with you. May you find hope, comfort, and compassion as you read this book and be inspired to create your own uplifted grief journey.

SECTION 1

Love Is Alive

> *"Two of the most remarkable days of my life were when I heard, 'Hi Mom, it's me', from each of my daughters in the afterlife decades apart. In both situations, my elation was off the charts as I received confirmation that my cherished child was safe. The peace it brought to me is indescribable as a mother while deep in the throes of devastating loss."*
>
> —*Nancy Yuskaitis*

Hi Mom, it's me. These four little words had the immense power to transform my life in truly miraculous ways—four little words with the healing energy to uplift and direct my grief journey forever. They were simple words, really, with a big impact that would light my path into the unknown and confirm that my daughter was alive and safe in the afterworld.

Unbelievably, this would happen not once but twice after the sudden and heartbreaking loss of both of my beautiful daughters, many decades apart. My prayers were answered at that moment, and I truly felt the sincerity and presence of each of them with me at the time, saying, *Hi, Mom, it's me. Don't worry. I am okay. I know you can't see me, but I am still with you, and I have much to share with you.*

In their own unique yet similar way, both of my girls provided reassurance through afterlife messages that were loving and kind, and that opened a doorway in my consciousness to the world between us.

It was just the beginning of a long and continuing heart-centered, soul-to-soul connection, mother to daughter, blending heaven and earth with each of them as individuals and united as the Soulful Starlights. In the following pages, I will share with you the ongoing communication that transpired between us, which lifted my grieving spirit from the heaviness of grief to one of shining light, comforted in their love.

Mom, I am with you, always. See me in the wind and in the wonderful ways I show you my continued presence with you in writing our story, in family gatherings, and in comforting you in your sorrow.

Blessed are those who can open their hearts to the presence of loved ones who guide their path from the other side. Our souls stay connected through eternity.

One
Between Two Worlds

"It seems so long ago that you were born. Although you are so close in heart, it feels timeless."

—**Nancy Yuskaitis**

M*om,*
I've missed you. I love you very much. All is well in the afterworld. Since I left at such a young age, I have a special bond with young souls. I am passionate about assisting them to adjust when they return to this realm. I understand what they go through when they first arrive back here. It is a rewarding experience as their hearts are so open. They just need a steady hand to lead them back to feeling safe again. ~ Lavender 2005

My daughter, Lavender, was my gateway to receiving afterlife communications.

As a young mom, losing her as an infant was incomprehensible. It was also shocking, heartbreaking, and cruel. The trauma of that day, along with the cold lack of empathy and support from the hospital staff and those closest to me, was transformative. The sudden and immense loss of her weighed heavily on my body, mind, and spirit for the following decade.

I couldn't see it clearly at the time, but later realized that this was my journey to experience and my responsibility to find healing from the heartbreak and shame so that I was capable of being the loving and emotionally present mother I dreamed of being to my family.

Each career path I chose always seemed to involve helping others in some way, and though it was rewarding, it was also very draining. At this point, I realized that I needed to look beyond what I had been to find healing and purpose in my life.

In the process, I became passionate about my spiritual development in my grief journey as I parented my firstborn, a son, and later my daughter, Crystal.

For nearly all my adult life, I have been a grieving mother, having experienced the devastating heartbreak of child loss at a very young age after my second child, Lavender, unexpectedly passed away in my arms as an infant due to a suspected heart defect.

In my grief, I sought confirmation that life continued after one's passing. I believed our souls live on, and I longed to know where my baby daughter's soul had gone. My heart desperately wanted to connect with her on a soul level, and I felt that her soul was loving and wise, wishing to communicate with me. I had read it was possible to receive a message from those in the afterlife. I just wasn't sure how to go about it.

I began by consuming every book I could find on life after life and afterlife communication. I attended spiritual classes, first in guided meditation in group settings, and later received my personal mantra in a transcendental meditation course, which prompted a daily meditation practice at home that continues to this day.

Meditation provided the doorway or portal through which I could listen to my intuition and was an introduction to my angels and spirit guides. Through their assistance, I became aware that my energy was indeed heavy and dripping with sadness, and my inner light was very dim. I was able to observe that my emotions had become flat and colorless without my realizing it, and I was numb, unable even to feel the emotion of joy.

All the unhealed trauma of early loss had taken its toll on my well-being, and I could feel it dragging on my spirit. Around the same time, a friend introduced me to Reiki's healing energy and encouraged me to participate in becoming certified in Reiki 1, which would facilitate my journey to renewed health and emotional wellness.

I will share more about my Reiki journey in a later chapter, but it has been and still is a part of my daily, soulful self-care. Day by day, layer by layer, I consciously began a process of letting go, lightening up, and freeing myself from the heavy weight of grief. I was mindful of it, even though I wasn't familiar with the term mindfulness at the time. This concentrated focus to heal my trauma was a personal journey that I shared with skilled and caring practitioners, such as massage therapists and energy workers, who helped to release the heavy grief my body was clutching onto.

As I progressed in my spiritual development, I began to let go of the protective shell that had developed around my heart, dampening down my intuition and emotions. This healing process allowed my heart to open in new, colorful, and radiant ways, enabling me to experience love and joy deeply, and my life felt transformed.

Two

Hope Brightens the Darkest Days

"Those we love don't go away. They live alongside us every day, offering love, compassion, and grace as we transform, heal, and grow."

—***Nancy Yuskaitis***

While I actively and consciously participated in my healing journey, I desperately longed to communicate with Lavender. Although I personally did not know anyone who could speak with those in the afterlife, I somehow believed it was possible.

It was through the contacts I made at the metaphysical center in Naples, Florida, that I was one day told about a young woman who offered channeling consultations and could help me connect with Lavender. Through my research, I learned about psychic mediums, and I was absolutely intrigued and interested in exploring the possibility of receiving a message from her.

Nervously, I arranged a session, and after a short wait, I was in this woman's living room, heart pounding with anticipation of what was to come. She began our session with a brief opening prayer and requested that my daughter or any relatives of mine come forth with messages for me. Almost immediately, my daughter, Lavender, began to communicate with her. She was so anxious and ready for this opportunity that was miraculously set up by the spirit world to reconnect us.

Through this medium, she said, *"Hi, Mom, it's me."*

Receiving those few words was incredible, and I truly felt my daughter's presence with me. The message she provided was simple, yet it marked the beginning of a long exchange of mother–daughter conversations between heaven and earth.

Leaving that session, I was on cloud nine. I couldn't have been more ecstatic. The realization that life continues after death and soul communication is possible was confirmed to me at that moment. It prompted me to increase my study and practice to open my channel to the spirit world so that I could communicate with my daughter myself.

Very soon after that session, I began to see angels around me in my daily life. One would often sit on my bed in the morning when I woke up, or I would catch one watching me from a distance while I worked. I found it extremely comforting that I was being guided, protected, and assisted from heaven to understand that I wasn't alone in my grief, and I certainly wasn't facing this challenging life alone.

My Catholic upbringing provided an awareness of guardian angels, and I was conscious of their protection as I grew up. I could sometimes see one in my room at night. I certainly felt protected in several traumatic incidents, including a boating accident where, as a very young child, I was called upon to save the lives of my dad, uncle, and cousins, being the only one not thrown off a motorboat stuck in gear that was spinning around them in circles. At that moment, as my Dad yelled to me in total panic, I was able to turn off the engine without instruction before any harm was done to my family. Although this event was never discussed with me again, I was later informed in meditation that it was due to the assistance of my angels, who guided me to turn off the engine so I could be safely reunited with my family.

In my teenage and young adult years, there were several times when I felt angelic protection around me. During one such moment, I was sitting in my car at my mother's home in Miami with my very young children, and bullets were fired at our car, flattening the tires. Even though this action was to scare me, the angels blocked those bullets from injuring us or traumatizing us further.

Later, as my children grew up, I'm sure their guardian angels played a role in protecting them from harm or in very dangerous situations. I am comforted that they were with Crystal at the time of her departure to the spirit world.

In our writing sessions, Lavender informed me that she would set off an alert for assistance from the angels at times when their presence is needed, where she works in the heavenly realm, tending to babies and children as they cross over. Although the angels are unable to prevent someone's passing, they are there to ease their way.

As I continued pursuing my practice of opening my channel to the spirit world, I began receiving messages from my paternal grandfather. His spirit's presence was comforting and real to me, and I would see him in my dreams and hear him in my meditations. One day, as I was walking on the beach in the Abaco Bahamas with my dad, he began to break down crying, a sight I had never seen before. When I asked him what he was feeling, he began to express how he still missed my grandfather every day in the nearly fifteen years since his passing. He said he was his best friend and greatest supporter. I believe that my grandfather was so closely tied to me at that time that my dad was overcome with emotion at feeling his dad's presence around us in that tender moment.

As my connection opened, the portal of communication allowed other souls in the afterlife to communicate with me. Friends of mine and loved ones of people I knew who had passed began contacting me with messages of their safe arrival on the other side. One of these friends was Chris, and he often attended classes on spiritual development with me in Naples, Florida. Prior to his becoming ill from cancer and leaving this plane of existence, we made a pact to contact each other if one went before the other. He kept his word and communicated with me right away in a loving and protective manner. He often sent messages in automatic writing to support and encourage the challenging situations we faced in dealing with Crystal's early childhood trauma.

As these experiences increased, I became aware that I was still carrying a heavy burden of sadness from losing Lavender, which weighed my spirit down from fully experiencing life. In my relationships on the earth plane, I was unable to share my pain as no one in my life at that time wanted to hear it or be supportive in any way, and I became pretty proficient at hiding my feelings and emotions. The beautiful souls on the other side, who knew me, could see my suffering and encourage healing on a deep, soul level.

At this point, I was being drawn to be supportive of other bereaved parents, and for a time, I became a co-facilitator at the local grief support group. I assisted by producing the newsletter for our chapter and helped lead meetings. As I listened to these parents, their children began visiting me in my dreams, bringing messages of hope and solace to comfort them. With their permission, I would share these messages. It was a beneficial way for me to honor Lavender's life, to be of service to families of loss, and to feel less alone.

After that one session with a medium, Lavender was communicating with me on a regular basis, soft and faint at first, but soon her voice came through strong and clear. Always starting with, *Hi, Mom, it's me.* I could feel her energy and recognize her presence as that of a beautiful soul offering love, respect, and compassion. When I was suffering, she would send out an alert for angels and spirit guides to comfort me with kindness and support.

Her encouragement from the heavenly realms has assisted in guiding and maintaining my perseverance to grow, expand, and evolve through my life experiences. She has given me instructions on how to let go of things I cannot change, to forgive, to accept, and to trust myself, all with the essence of unconditional love, light, and immense compassion. Her introduction to afterlife communication with me has been the most transformative experience I could have imagined, and I am forever grateful for her dedication and persistence all these years.

Lavender Love[1]

As a young woman
barely out of my teens
married to my first love
a delighted mom of a darling boy
elated by the birth of a precious girl
The dawn of that summer day
my life shattered into eternity
Nestled in my arms
my light-eyed baby lay
when the sun began to rise, I wept
my beautiful girl
had silently slipped away
leaving us to carry her loss every day
Years would pass by in deep heartache
her older brother would bring comfort
and her younger sister would bring joy
yet, the longing for her never faded away
Life changed again and again
in divorce and remarriage
when mystical channels of soul
communication occurred
I realized my baby girl was not gone
she was alive and well in
another realm

---

[1] *All poems and quotes used in this book are originals of the author, Nancy Yuskaitis.*

Three
Into the Light

"Life has not been the same without you. Please stay with me, at least for a while. My heart aches for you, and my mind can't conceptualize that you are really gone. It doesn't seem possible that our story on earth is over."

—*Nancy Yuskaitis*

Crystal with eyes as blue as the ocean, her lighthearted way comforts as she inspires in self-love and self-compassion.

When my daughter Crystal left this world decades after her sister, my life was turned upside down again, and I struggled to find my way in an unfortunate yet slightly familiar new reality. My grief felt unbearable as if I was living in a dense fog that I couldn't see my way out of. My only desire at the time was to receive confirmation that she, like her sister, had landed safely in the afterworld.

This time, however, it didn't take years before I knew; it was only a matter of days because she knew it was possible, and so did I. We just needed to clear the channel that was covered in dense grief and a cloud of confusion. She kept trying to communicate, and as soon as the grief lifted enough, she was able to get through to me. Her messages also began loud and clear with, *Hi, Mom, it's me.* With tears streaming down my face, I was not only ecstatic but also immensely relieved.

As you will see throughout this book, our story is a bit unique in that both of my daughters are bonded in the afterlife, supporting me in all I do and hope to do, along with a team of angels and spirit guides offering soulful inspired adventures and mystical, magical and mindful messages prompting my acceptance of the love being showered on me.

It is quite beautiful to see the connection between them and how aligned, yet different, they are, having never lived on earth at the same time. Their combined effort to pull me out of the darkness and into the light-filled world where they lived while I resided on earth was life-changing.

Throughout Crystal's life on earth, she looked to me to be her lighthouse, strong, empowering, and filled with strength as she tried to heal from things she couldn't speak of. After her passing, she became my beacon of light, brightening my path through loss to live a life of reclaimed joy and adventures while encouraging my journey to illuminate the path for others in mediumship, spiritual life coaching, and in writing this book.

Four
Gone without Goodbye

"When I think of you, I realize that you're not doing any of the things I usually imagine you doing throughout the day. Now, when I think of you, I must imagine what you are doing in heaven."

—*Nancy Yuskaitis*

My bright, bubbly, blue-eyed daughter lived for two decades on an addiction train before it crashed the final and last time. I boarded that train with her hundreds of times to support, console, encourage, empower, love, and offer healing during its journey into the light of rebirth and to the depths of emotional darkness. It was immensely painful for each of us as we cared about the other's well-being and valued our relationship throughout her life. Her stepdad and I were available to her in her struggles and her triumphs, and we feel confident she felt our support as she gave her best efforts to overcome a complicated life of trauma beginning at birth.

Her joys of improved well-being were contagious and overflowed with hope and promise, only to be met face-to-face with the harsh reality of relapse again and again. Watching your child or loved one struggle with addiction is so terrifying that, in some protective way, I was practicing my own version of soulful self-care and self-preservation emotionally while remaining immensely hopeful for her recovery. Many of the soulful, inspired practices that I share here—I implemented in my life during those decades when life was out of control for both of us and somehow translated into finding peace, comfort, and reclaimed joy when none existed after her passing.

On the day I received the sudden and unexpected confirmation from my husband and son that she was gone, my heart was shattered into a million pieces, and my world fell apart. It was a crushing and devastating pain, and I screamed as I fell to the floor, feeling as if I had been stabbed in the heart. Every breath I took was excruciatingly painful. The weight of grief pressed heavily on my chest. My sobbing was so loud and intense that it enveloped me, and I couldn't speak or hear anything other than the sound of my own sorrow.

In the following days, I grieved moment to moment, pondering my desire to go on living, and I cried out to my late daughter, *Why did you leave?, Where are you?,* and *How could you leave without saying goodbye?* My heart ached for an answer, but I didn't expect it right then. When I cried uncontrollably, my husband held me in his arms with loving empathy. I was emotionally and physically drained and needed a comforting place to lie down in my sorrow. Yet, I knew from personal experience that hearing from her in spirit was the only relief I could receive to ease my broken heart.

As each of us experiences a loss differently, those closest to us need to offer patience and compassion as we grieve. This kindness will go a long way in protecting the marriage or family ties in this emotionally charged time. I needed to hear from her. It was that simple. She knew it was possible; she was very intuitive, and I felt she would try to reach me as soon as I could receive it. But when would that be?

In my experience, the messages I receive from loved ones and others on the other side come through more easily when I'm in a calm and centered emotional state, not necessarily when I'm overwhelmed or distraught. I prayed for peace and the acceptance of a loss I didn't want to accept. Through my tears, I called out to life: *Why, why must I endure the loss of another child? Why must my precious daughters both leave me here to grieve?* I also wanted to know why people die at the time they do.

I was certain that Crystal was fully aware of my ability to listen to the souls of those who had crossed over, and as far back as she could remember, I had been communicating with her older sister, Lavender. I called out to her: *Please let me know you are okay.*

My world had turned dark. Losing her to an accidental overdose meant no more second chances, fresh starts, or new beginnings. Suddenly, life became a blur of unanswered questions, sorrow, regret, and disbelief. *How could this happen?* I asked her again and again. *If only I could have done more, if only I could have protected you when you were hurt as a child at a neighbor's home, you wouldn't have escaped into numbing your pain through drugs and alcohol.*

She waited twenty years to share with me that she had been physically violated. All those years, she kept it inside, trying to push it away, but the trauma would always return. Counseling, rehab, recovery groups, and halfway houses all helped, but there was no cure.

If only I could have protected her from relapsing on that evening when she took her last breath. If only I could have changed the direction of her life to a healthier path. If only I were there to hold her hand when she slipped away. I had so many regrets, yet none of those things were in my control or power to direct. All I could really do was love her unconditionally, and I absolutely did.

While my life felt upended entirely by this traumatic loss, I trusted that I could find solace by writing my experiences in a journal and listening for guidance from the spirit world. I had learned many years ago after Lavender's passing that combining meditation with journaling in the form of automatic writing was one of my survival tools and could be used as a healthy way to pour out my painful emotions, articulate my feelings, process my grief, and receive guidance, support, and encouragement from the spirit world, including angels, guides and loved ones.

It is in that space that I would gain access to the messages from beyond and receive ongoing confirmation that love and life continue beyond death and that our souls never die. It was in the process of journaling, combined with meditation that I began to hear my daughter, Crystal, express to me everything that I needed and wanted to know to integrate her loss and survive it. The messages and signs I've received in the hours, days, and years that followed have provided immense comfort, compassion, and confirmation that communication with our loved ones is absolutely possible. They are always lovingly watching over us and encouraging us to transform, heal, and grow.

She's Gone

My grown daughter is gone
she has left my world for another
my two daughters are now together
leaving me heartbroken
I can barely lift myself out of bed
my body is feeling ten times heavier
I can barely lift my arms
my legs are weak
energy is deflated
I am listless

Gone without Goodbye

If only I was there to say goodbye
the day my youngest slipped away
I would have held her hand
kissed her cheek
and hugged her one last time
The sorrow would be immense
that this lifetime together
was coming to an end
Love and light would fill the room
as my heart expressed
the gift she was to me
Apologies would be given for ways
I couldn't protect her
no matter how I tried
Lamenting would take place
about the faces of addiction
and how she gave her very best
to overcome and heal
A little laughter in our usual way
could be heard as we remembered
her crazy antics and
all that she survived
Tears would fill an ocean
as I let go and
her spirit and soul would lift
to the skies, wild and free
A spiritual bond would remain
and a pact would be made
to connect with me when
she found her heavenly resting place

Five

The First Hello

➤〰〰〰

"Not a day will go by for the rest of my life where I don't miss you and wish you were here."

—Nancy Yuskaitis

My intense desire to connect with my daughter immediately after I received the news of her passing grew stronger with each moment. Yet even though I had been practicing mediumship for many years, when sorrow is so fresh and grief so deep, it can block communication from the spirit world. I couldn't receive her messages, though she tried. As with Lavender, a friend mentioned a medium to assist who had helped her when her son passed away. As soon as we opened the session, Crystal was there waiting to share her message with me through this medium.

Her bubbly enthusiasm rang through, and I knew at that moment that all was well in her new world. Her only concern was for my well-being. She stated that she was with Lavender, and my former pets, including dogs, a bird, and a bunny or two, surrounded them. She expressed gratitude for this medium's assistance as my grief was so heavy she had difficulty breaking through it with her messages of love and confirmation of her place in the afterlife. It was an exquisitely beautiful experience and a wonderful reunion as both my daughters were right there, reassuring me of their love from heaven.

A few days after my session, when Crystal tried again, she was able to get through, and I received the message I had been hoping for, praying for, and asking for, and it came loud, vibrant, and clear.

Hi, Mom, It's me. I'm here. I love you. I'm okay. Lavender's here, too. We send our love. Please try not to be so sad. I'm okay. Please do not worry. My suffering and struggle have come to an end. It was a peaceful passing. I am in a good place in my mind and heart, surrounded by loved ones, like at a reunion.

After that, our connection became clear and open, and mother–daughter time became a daily occurrence in my life. I would sit first thing in the morning and gaze at the mountain view in our backyard in Mt. Crested Butte, Colorado, at sunrise, with my coffee in hand, and listen, writing down what was shared with me, asking questions, and jotting down the answers in my journal.

To say I was bursting with joy is an understatement. *OMG! She's here and she's alright. WOW.* I was in a state of bliss, and it was amazing. The sound of Crystal's voice came through exactly as she was, with all the same intensity, language, and personality of her life on earth. The only difference I could sense was that she was now the one offering immense love, compassion, and nurturing to me, as if the roles were reversed.

Let yourself be filled with peace and comforted in the knowledge that you, as a parent, did the best you could to guide my life. However, free will kept me from having to recirculate some lessons again and again, and I know that was wearing on you. I never meant to hurt you or any of my family or friends, and I will forever be grateful for the role each of you played in my life story.

It was unbelievable. Wow! Her bright and caring spirit was right with me, soothing my emotions and lightening my grief, and I could feel her holding me as I cried. Hearing her voice reassuring me that *all is well in her world* was all I needed, and for that, I was tearfully relieved and oh so very grateful.

Crystal's Second Message

Today, I realized something important in my grief journey. It is a time when my daughter is no longer struggling, but my journey of suffering has just begun. My eyes stung from all the weeping that wouldn't stop, and I found that lying down in meditation with my eyes closed felt soothing to my body, mind, and soul. It really didn't matter to me what the weather was outside because I was too teary to leave my bed. I felt comfort in the quiet warmth of my room with the shades closed as I withdrew from this life and allowed myself to listen to messages from the other side.

Each day, as I grieved in quiet contemplation, I sought relief from my sorrow through the support of my guardian angels and my daughters in the spirit world, who assisted in healing the wounds of my broken heart. It would take a collaborative effort from myself, friends, family, and the immense support and guidance I received from the other side to carry me forward in healing and sharing this journey with you.

Mom, I want you to know I love you very much, and I am here with you. Never lose faith in that. I will always be there for you. Yes, it is different now, of course, but my big heart still loves you and our family, and I am watching over you all. Life is sometimes the craziest thing to understand while we are living it, but you must allow yourself to trust in the process. My time on earth was over, and there was nothing you could have done to prevent my leaving. Saying goodbye would have been gut-wrenching for us both.

There was no time for a peaceful goodbye, no time for a gentle goodbye, and no option for you to hold my hand as I slipped away. It was something I had to do alone. I know you're aware of how much I've never liked being alone, but this was my time to experience it. Although it seemed that no one was with me at the time of my passing, your loving daughter and my big sister, Lavender, was with me. I could feel her presence, and I could see that she was holding out her hand toward me in my final moment. I was not afraid. Of course, my guardian angels were there with us, too.

When I saw my sister, I immediately thought of you and how it would break your heart. Before I knew it, she beckoned me to follow her, to take her hand, and to leave all my earthly troubles for a new life of peace and freedom from my addictions.

"What about Mom?" I asked. She nodded compassionately and answered, "She'll understand."

I had no choice but to believe her. I dropped everything I held so dear and let my spirit soar high above my body. My first days in this new realm were tumultuous, just as yours on earth, but I always remembered that you could communicate with people who had crossed over. I knew I just had to try to reach you as soon as possible.

Your grief was so dense that we needed a translator that first time, but within a few days, our vibrations were synced up to exchange love, emotion, and messages to comfort you.

I understand it's hard to accept from where you are, but please work toward finding peace within the physical loss of my presence on earth. I know your heart aches, and it hurts terribly. Let light wash over you and soothe you. Let yourself be comforted by the natural beauty of your surroundings, and let the spirit world guide you to the next step. Our relationship will continue forever.

We love and adore you, Mom. You can rest assured of that.

By the Sea

"Sit by the sea and know I am sitting with you.
Talk to me. I can hear you.
Know that I am always trying to amaze and delight you with patterns in the sky and unexpected signs and surprises.
Be aware that life is filled with remarkable, awe-inspiring experiences that give you a moment to pause in gratitude."

—Crystal from the Afterlife

Receiving these few messages felt like a healing balm had washed over my heart and soul, bringing an abundance of love, compassion, empathy, and support from not just one but both of my daughters in the heavenly realm. Crystal was front and center as her loss was so recent in guiding my grief process with direct messages designed to heal. Many nights and early mornings, she would awaken me with a gentle nudge, saying *Mom, wake up and write.* It was through these automatic writing sessions that I received the heartfelt hope necessary to guide my survival of child loss for the second time. Other times, when I was intensely longing for her or was having a heavy bout of crying, she would come close and comfort me with, *Mom, I'm here for you.*

Let Go and Shine

Let your pain, go
Let your sadness, grief and feelings of loss, go
Allow your being to be filled with light
Allow love to permeate all that you are and all that you do
Allow full expression in your life
Allow peace and wellness to fill your body
Allow your connection to spirit to deepen and widen
Allow your soul to heal
Allow your spirit to shine

Crystal's Third Message

Mom, I love you very much. I could always feel your love for me, but having the separation at the end with you not being there made my transition easier in leaving you.

Our bond was such that we could read and feel each other's joy and pain, and we were quite emotionally dependent on each other. I needed time to disconnect from you for a bit before making this transition; otherwise, it would have been unbearable, and I might have been stuck between two worlds. Just know that I never stopped loving you for a second in life, but my suffering and struggle have come to an end.

Baby, my heart is breaking, but my elation is off the charts in hearing from you. Please stay close and share with me all that is needed for my well-being to survive your loss. I don't know how to live without your presence in my life.

Crystal's Fourth Message

Mom, I'm okay, really. More okay than I ever was on earth. But I miss you. It's not fair for you to be so sad and hurt this much. I will do what I can to comfort you. You have my word. I wish you didn't have to suffer through this pain, and I'm sorry for all I've put you through. I know you only wanted the best for me. It's all going to be okay; you'll see. I will live forever in your heart. You will go on to live life experiencing joy and knowing that I will be by your side. Let yourself live, let yourself laugh, and take in all the love that is being sent to you.

Crystal, I am grateful for your strong presence, tenacity, and intensity. I miss that so much. Thank you for walking this path with me in all the ways you do and for assisting in helping me to see the beauty and light in life as the darkness gives way to renewal and hope.

Crystal's Fifth Message

My big heart still loves you and our family, and I am watching over you all. I know your heart aches. Let yourself find something, even the littlest thing to be grateful for, especially while you are in pain and longing for things to be different. I know you miss my big personality, my warm hugs, and the protectiveness that I offered you. I know you will always miss me, and I can't believe that our life together is over. Let your tears flow when they need to. Let your emotions out. Don't keep them inside. Take extra special care of yourself. You are grieving, and your life will never be the same.

"Live in a way that you can be proud of when you die. Live with no regrets. Live life with gusto and enthusiasm. Go for it. Whatever you want to do, to be, to experience." ~ Crystal from the Afterlife

Message for the Grieving

Give yourself space to mourn.
Allow the loving gestures of others to comfort you.
Express kindness and compassion to yourself and others.
Accept invites from friends and family whenever possible.
May peace surround you all the days of your life.

Six
Waking Up on the Other Side

"Life is pure energy, and the exchange between us and the spirit realm is exquisite and true."

—**Nancy Yuskaitis**

I *felt my angels around and family members beckoning me toward a lighted hallway, and before I knew it, I was consumed by the light as I was being guided by two guardian angels, one on each side of me. They instructed me to let go and not fear the unknown of what was ahead of me. They also encouraged me to let go of any worry about leaving my life behind, that there would be time soon to recount my life and relationships and to be in touch with you.*

My first intention was my concern for you: what will you think, how will you find out, who will comfort you in your sorrow? My angels told me it would all be taken care of and not to worry. As I slipped away, I could see my body, yet I did not feel any physical pain. I observed others attending to me in shock and disbelief and then in practical terms.

As for my other belongings, there wasn't much, and it was spread all over. You have the meaningful pieces I left, and of course, you have me. I love you now and forever.

When I entered my new home, a place they call heaven, it was just like waking up on the other side of the world. What a beautiful world it is, and I would like to describe it to you.

As the days turned to a new month, the writing sessions between us intensified and began to be known as the Soulful Starlight Sessions.

I now live in peace, surrounded by loved ones, children, and pets. My life feels good, and I am smiling all the time. Please know I am with you more now than I was in my earthly life. Just think of me or call my name, and I am there right by your side. Feel me in your home, our home, and I am there. My heart and soul are there. Wherever you are, I am there too. When you are smiling, I am smiling too. Feel me hugging and holding you when you cry. I notice how much you cherish each gift and greeting card I gave you and how you saved them throughout the years. I will continue to send gifts to you from this beautiful place where I now live.

Do you realize how blessed we are that we can continue to communicate in this way? When there is separation in the way of death, our feelings for our loved ones still exist, but many signs and efforts to communicate are not received.

Just as I was writing this chapter, I was startled out of my chair by a large bluebird that flew up and banged on the glass door beside me, then glided up to sit in a nearby tree. I will take that as a sign that Crystal is writing with me as I tell her story.

"Baby, I need to hear from you. Please tell me what you can. I'm struggling here without you."

I'm okay. Really, more than I was on earth. But I miss you, and I know you love me. Please try to get it together. It's not fair for you to be so sad and hurting so much. I will do what I can to comfort you. You have my word. I've got your back. As you can tell right now, my energy can transmit to you perfectly. I can avail myself of your surroundings in the way of surprise experiences to delight and make you smile. Let yourself LIVE and let yourself LAUGH and take in all the LOVE that is being shown to you. Know that this is not your fault. I wish you didn't have to go through all the pain. I am so sorry for all I have put you through.

Life was crazy for me and very difficult, and in my ignorance, I made many wrong or unhelpful decisions for myself. I know you only wanted the best for me, and I felt I could never live up to those standards. My lessons were more than I could bear or handle or rise above. Don't feel sorry that we didn't get one last time together before my time ran out. I thought I would have more time. It's going to be okay; you'll see. I will live forever in your heart as the happy-go-lucky girl I once was as a child. I am still the same, only better. My moodiness is gone, my depression has lifted, and my insecurities are no longer a part of me, but what remains is my desire to help others.

I enjoy giving of my energy to assist, to uplift, and to protect those whose care I am entrusted with. You will recover and go on to live a long, healthy, happy life. I will always be by your side, watching over you and guiding you in the most nurturing and loving manner possible. It's my turn to nurture you, and although you can't see me, I am here for you. I will always be. I have done much healing work, schooling, and lessons in this afterworld to heal my soul, and I want very much to be there to collaborate with you on art and writing to free your soul from the restraints of child loss, twice and to assist in any way I can.

Lavender is with me and sends her immense love for you. She has obviously a different life experience and perspective than I do, and she has been guiding your life for many decades with love and care. I know you asked her to watch over me many times, and although she did do so, it was my unstable free will that kept getting in the way.

Time is different here. But love is love, and we are free to watch over our loved ones and comfort them in times of sorrow. Do not mourn my loss; be grateful for the bond we shared. That will never go away. Instead of looking forward to seeing me, talking on the phone, or exchanging cards and letters, look forward to communicating with me in this way. My adjustment has been easier than your acceptance of it. I am surrounded by light and loving beings filled with compassion, generosity, and warmth who have guided me in a new way of living.

I am grateful for all the loving spirits around you on earth and in heaven who are also assisting you in this major life change. Please let go of your attachment to me on earth and know that I am free to fly in a joyful new world that I will share with you in our Soulful Starlight Sessions. I hope you feel the love and admiration I send to you for always loving and supporting me through light and darkness. I will always be grateful. Much love and comfort to you now and always.

Crystal

A Quieter Life

My world isn't the same place anymore
life seems empty and quieter somehow
so much is missing now that you're gone
although in my mind I know you're not far

My heart still cries over the loss of you
I know you had to go; your time here was done
yet I'll never stop longing to see you again

No one will ever take your place in my life
there is, and always will be just one you

My days are filled with passion and purpose
there's work, friendships, and loved ones to see
there's rarely a moment my thoughts aren't of you

Missing your calls, letters, and texts
I'll reread the treasured ones again and again
looking for answers and signs from you

I'll gaze at your picture with heartache and loss
memories swirl about while longing is felt

Life goes on, yes that's true
I'll never forget you, please don't drift away
stay with me, stay with me, and hold my hand
as you walk this grief journey along with me

SECTION 2

Meet the Soulful Starlights

> *"Light is streaming down to you from the heavens through holes in the night sky known as stars."*
>
> —*Nancy Yuskaitis, Soulful Starlights*

They left this earth for the heavenly realms many decades apart, and although they had never lived on earth at the same time, their souls recognized each other as sisters.

Lavender: A sweet and vibrant energy in a short-lived life on earth. Her mission is to open hearts and allow for the exchange of love to uplift souls in this world. Her personality emits compassion, empathy, self-love, generosity, acceptance, protection, nature's beauty, and joy. In the afterlife, she lovingly works with children who cross over, helping them to adjust to their new environment.

Crystal: A ray of sunshine in a complicated life filled with hope and despair, kindness and separation, promise and pain, empathy, compassion, and love. She possesses the ability to lift people up with her effervescent personality, smile, and emotions. Her mission is to provide a loving presence that is lighthearted and playful, creating the awareness of wonder, delight, and enjoyment through creativity, unexpected surprises, and soulful, inspired adventures. In the afterlife, she works with those who cross over due to addiction as she relates to the circumstances they face in this new environment.

Two bright and beautiful shining stars of my life who are filled with wisdom, compassion, lightness, and love.

The first time I was given the awareness of the Soulful Starlights was by an angel who works closely with me while I was in a meditative writing session one day. She stated, *I am here to usher in your Soulful Starlights, who have much to share with you.*

Almost immediately, she showed me a scene of Crystal as a young girl at a candle-lighting ceremony in memory of her older sister, Lavender, whom she had never met. It then flashed back in my thoughts of this time with the child loss group that I was involved in for a while in Naples, Florida. We were there as a family, and my two children had joined me at this event.

Within a few moments, Crystal began to express that after that day, she began to feel Lavender's presence around her and developed her own relationship with her. She believed she could always count on her sister to watch over her and to come close in times of pain or suffering.

When it was my time to leave the earth, I was delighted, relieved, and felt so protected by Lavender, who took my hand as I crossed over into the afterworld to join with my guardian angel, who took my other hand. When I hesitated to leave this earth, knowing how painful it would be for you to lose another child, Lavender gave her permission to go by, assuring me that you would not only be alright in time but grateful that we were united. The guardian angels would work alongside you in mediumship and in sharing love, light, hope, and compassion with the world.

As I was introduced to this united team, the message came through as follows.

We are your Soulful Starlights, your Starlight, Starbright girls. We are your guiding lights along this adventure in life and the afterlife, here to strengthen, energize, and assist those grieving the loss of a loved one. Together, we are messengers of love and light being sent to you to comfort and guide you on your soul's journey. It is our intention to provide encouragement and support as you walk a healing path.

Quickly, they formed a united bond and began to communicate with me individually and as a pair when I needed their strength and willpower to go on in life without them. The exchange between us is exquisite and true, and my light shines so brilliantly because of their loving presence in my life. I truly feel as if I've experienced a miracle of transforming my devastatingly heavy grief into a softer, lighter, gentler grief through this experience, which is why I wanted to share this story with you.

Seven

Soulful Starlight Sessions

———≫—

"Stay centered, stay strong, soak in the beauty of nature, and allow yourself to be transformed in the process. Don't ever let your sparkle be dimmed by your disappointment in how others respond to your grief process. Not everyone is meant to feel the way you do, and that's okay. Let your light shine, anyway."

—Nancy Yuskaitis, *Soulful Starlights*

The Soulful Starlight Sessions always began with a request: *Mom, we need to talk,* or *Mom, it's me,* and that was my cue to sit with my laptop or journal to record them. Often, the messages are given on a specific topic or regarding a particular situation that could benefit from guidance, insight, and healing. They may be conversational in style, and I can and do respond by expressing or asking questions. Other times, the messages are given on a variety of topics such as wellness, creativity, the healing arts, mindfulness, self-love, reclaiming joy, kindness, affirmations, and blessings.

Mom, we are here with messages from the heavens to those who are ready to receive them. It is for anyone who has lost a loved one or is curious about the afterlife.

Heaven is filled with many souls who seek to assist earthbound souls whose ties remain through the separation. Everywhere you go, you have a team of angels, spirit guides, and loved ones supporting, protecting, and encouraging you. You will see your loved ones again. Until that time, it is important to live out your life knowing they are by your side, encouraging you in every step and stumble you take to regain hope, joy, and love for life again.

May you be inspired to trust the journey with an open heart and a spirit full of adventure. We are here with you. Never doubt our presence. In this world, on the other side, we delight in supporting, encouraging, and assisting those on the earth plane and are available to help each of you to evolve, heal, and grow.

We will share with you the beauty of both realms. There are some similarities. Life on earth is a school of lessons that introduce you to a higher consciousness if you are paying attention. Life is mystical and magical, but many on earth have forgotten to look at it in this manner. In the afterlife, everything feels expressive and truly judgment-free. There are many levels where other light-filled beings are consciously creating environments designed for learning, healing, and sharing compassion that exists without boundaries.

All are welcome to join in on this co-creation afterlife. Whatever your interest, there is a place where it is being explored and experienced. Life here takes on new meaning. There is no competition, as everyone's energy is fully realized. We all live out our purpose as equals with a similar intention of benefiting the universe. There is graciousness and pure love that radiates from one being to another. The energy is so elevated that in every direction you turn, the path is illuminated.

What a wonderful concept for us all. What if you started down a path into the unknown, and it suddenly became illuminated with clear light and focus? Would you take it as a positive sign and continue even though you could only see the beginning of the path? Would you trust yourself to follow this adventure wherever it might lead? Would you feel empowered to proceed boldly, or would you turn back to a familiar place?

In the afterlife, there is no wrong pathway. They all can lead to fulfillment. What if you could live more fearlessly on earth? Imagine the chances you would take if there were no wrong choices. The choice is yours.

Live your dreams; they are not as far away as you think. Believe, believe, believe. In any moment of doubt, relax and rely. I've got your back.

Life beyond Loss

Stay neutral with those who are unloving, for they are teachers on your life journey.

When you feel a lack of compassion, give compassion immensely.

When you feel lonely, reach out to brighten someone's day.

When you feel sad, let nature's beauty lighten your heart and share that light.

Act as if everything you say, do, and think matters because it most certainly does.

Allow the love in your heart to soften your edges of shattered dreams.

Allow the heartache to be transmuted into passion and purpose for lifting others up.

Share your strength, your soulful resilience, and your heart.

Allow kindness and self-love to radiate through you in soulful self-care.

Sparkle. Shine. Radiate Light.

Eight
Life in Another Realm

"Life is a wonder for those who look upon it as such."

—*Nancy Yuskaitis,* ***Soulful Starlights***

Did you know we have a beach view and can go here and look out at the sea?

We also have mountain vistas and deserts and countryside. Each soul is more comfortable in certain surroundings, like on earth. You can choose which environment you want to be in. Your in-laws are lakeside, just like on earth. Our dad and grandfathers are fishing in their own environments during their free time.

What do we do here, you ask? We comfort returning souls to be re-aligned to their surroundings again, to realize they have completed their lessons of that lifetime, and to integrate what those are. It is a way to expand one's soul's evolution to one of peace and purpose. There are numerous realms and divisions within each area, making it quite complex.

Allow the love in your heart for us to soften your grief. Let the longing you feel be lightened and shared in a safe community. Let the heartache you feel be transmuted into passion and purpose for lifting *others up. Imagine a swirl of kindness and self-care as it radiates through you, healing your pain and allowing your purpose to shine through the grief. Let your heart shine within to heal and to share it with the world.*

Experiencing confirmation that your loved ones are still with you through your grief has a profound effect and one that leads to greater awareness of the blending that occurs between heaven and earth. These messages are truly gifts from heaven that soothed my soul, healed my shattered heart, and uplifted my body, mind, and spirit beyond loss.

Mom, we are here with you. Never doubt our presence. In this world, on the other side, we delight in supporting, encouraging, and assisting our loved ones and others on the earth plane. It is our true desire to be of assistance now as we have been through our reviews, taken in our lessons, gone over and over the rights and wrongs of our life decisions, and looked closely at how we lived our lives. My life here now is beautiful. I am floating on clouds in peace and joy over the sense of freedom I feel in letting go of my earthly life.

Life is about experiencing the joys and complexities at the same time. It is noticing the subtle details and hanging on when the journey gets rough. It is about appreciating love and feeling gratitude, yet also about letting go of painful relationships and experiences. Life can take your breath away in awe of its beauty, yet it can also be devastatingly sad. Take time to rejoice in celebration when it is called for, and hold tight to those you love while you have them. Let love be exchanged among us on earth and in heaven, always.

Nine
A Life Review in Two Worlds

"Heaven, to me, is not a faraway place. It's a remarkable part of my everyday world. I find myself living in that in-between space between Mother Earth and the paradise in the sky. Often, I float away in conversation with those who have gone to live there."

—***Nancy Yuskaitis***

You are reliving many chapters in my life, and so am I. Let yourself find something to be grateful for each day while you are in pain and longing for things to be different. My life was full of adventure, maybe not the kind that most people strive for, but I made the most of the unusual situations I found myself in. I never wasted time in feeling sorry for myself. I always looked at how I could be of service in the here and now. My strength was in rising to the top of my painful situations with tenacity and a joyful spirit. It allowed me to endure what would be a depressing life for others and to be one of spiritual growth and service.

I always felt better when I was helping others and working toward a common goal. Could I have used my talents in different ways, you ask? Yes, but my life's lessons needed to take place in ways that were hard for you to understand. Remarkably, even in my so-called dysfunctional lifestyle, I touched the lives of many people who needed a spark of light that I could provide. My enthusiasm and energy could change the energy of the place wherever I went. Frequently, I got a charge out of uplifting others; it's where I derived my self-esteem and self-worth, and at other times, as an empath, it was draining, and I needed to rest and recharge.

Life was challenging for me, and I longed for more closeness with my family. I was not crazy or selfish. I was just overwhelmed by carrying the burden of my life's experiences. I was angry at times. However, I never meant to take it out on you. I was angry with myself for the abuse I suffered as a child, and no matter how much treatment or therapy I received, the self-loathing and contempt I felt would sabotage any peace or balance I had achieved in my life. I'm sorry for taking you on such an exhausting ride with highs and lows and long periods of discomfort for you. I tried; I really did. I gave my life all I had to give it. I know you wish I could have stayed with you forever, and you can't really believe it's over.

Let your tears flow when they need to, let your emotions out, don't keep them inside. Take extra special care of yourself, you are grieving, and life will never be the same. Allow yourself the space to heal and grow. Let yourself be comforted by the loving gestures of those who care about you. Let your emotions move through you, and let your sadness and tears float away. Give kindness and compassion to yourself and those around you. Accept invitations to join friends in laughter and dancing. May peace surround you all the days of your life.

Always, Crystal.

A soul's energy is timeless and not bound by the same standards of scheduling as on earth. Very soon after one passes, there is a life review that looks at your many life lessons, decisions, how we loved, how we cared for others, and how we gave of ourselves to people, places, and causes dear to our hearts. During this review and for some time afterward, it is brought to our attention how we hurt others, especially those we love. Our judgment, our mistrust, our selfishness, dishonesty, neglect, or abuse are all played out for us. We listen, feel, and learn about how our choices, actions, and behaviors affect others in our lives. While we are on earth, we think we are doing our best with the highest of intentions, and yet still, we are unaware of the consequences our life choices have on others. Some people live their lives looking out for themselves, while others look out for others, including animals and the planet. Yet, all do so in ways that may ignore their inner guidance on what may be best for them and all concerned.

Soulful Starlight Healing

> *"AFFIRMATION: I allow light-filled stars to fill my heart with love and joy, opening it from its current "closed again" status. I breathe in the experience of wellness, and I rise feeling refreshed and peaceful to begin anew."*
>
> **—*Nancy Yuskaitis***

On the morning after the second anniversary of Crystal's Celebration of Life, I awoke with an ache in my heart and a sadness that permeated my being. I closed my eyes and began to meditate. I took a few deep breaths and exhaled fully. As I focused on my breath, I could sense that my energy was very heavy and dense, and I felt crippled by a combination of regret and helplessness as a parent. I could tell immediately that this was going to be a tough morning. It had become a regular practice of mine to observe my state of mind and emotions at the beginning of each day and assess my approach to healing at that given time.

On certain days, sometimes Reiki energy, meditation, chakra balancing, prayer, self-talk, visualization, writing, physical activity, or simple mindfulness helped me to raise my spirits, disperse the heavy emotions, and clear the way for my heart to feel loved. As I placed my attention on being open to releasing the grief that weighed heavily on my chest, I could feel the presence of my Soulful Starlights as their souls came close to me, showering my energy field with golden light that felt like rain from the heavens in the form of light of a thousand stars. As I continued to meditate, I observed these stars that began to swirl around my body with a gentle healing energy. They allowed me to reopen my heart, which had been closed again, with the exquisite essence of starlight love.

Soulful Starlight Gift

"The night sky brings with it wisdom from the stars and is bestowed upon those who open their hearts to receive it. Life's journey may be lightened by a love that emanates from the Soulful Starlights in the night sky. They are filled with love for you so that you may realize that you are never alone. May this universal light fill your soul with renewed energy and strength as you heal and strive to live in peace. You may call on this light from the universe anytime you are feeling weary from the burdens you are carrying. May radiant light and joy shine upon you, uplifting and balancing your heart and soul."

—***Soulful Starlights***

Ten

You Are Not Alone

―⫸―

"My heartbreak of child loss has its blessings, too, in the continued support of my daughters in spirit and a gift of spirituality that is deep-rooted."

—*Nancy Yuskaitis*

This chapter will show you how our loved ones in heaven can and do assist us in our darkest moments, including some experiences in your life that can only be described as surreal. They are one-of-a-kind, once-in-a-lifetime heart-bursting experiences that are filled with profound sadness combined with a beauty that takes your breath away. A moment when time stands frozen in place, where there is an understanding that is tender and raw between a mother and her child, husband and wife, or other close relations. In my own life, I have one with each of my daughters that stands above all the other beautiful, heartfelt, and tragic memories that transported me to a place of awe and immense gratitude for the strength I was given to rise above the heartbreak and observe the beauty in the bittersweet.

Life is about experiencing the joys and complexities at the same time. It will take your breath away in awe of its beauty, and yet it can also take your breath away in devastating sadness.

Beauty in the Bittersweet: Lavender Love

When my sweet Lavender was laid to rest as an infant, we chose a beautiful little pink casket, and her grandmas and great-grandmas arrived in spring-colored dresses on that warm summer day. The memory of it is so tragic and so long ago that it is a blur to me now, but I do know it was in a family gravesite, deep in the city of my hometown of Miami, Florida. Through the years following her sudden passing, I was grateful to feel her spirit presence with me, so I didn't feel the pressure to go to the cemetery to talk with her or feel a closeness with her. I knew she was just a thought away. When I wanted to acknowledge her in a special way, I would bring flowers into my home, create art in her memory, or write a letter to her and receive her response in my automatic writing. I would also give messages of comfort to others who had lost a loved one.

Decades later, when my mother passed away, I arranged for a new headstone with both of their names listed on it. Still, I never imagined what would take place as our immediate family gathered at the gravesite for my mother's ceremony. It was also Lavender's resting place because she had offered to share it with her all those years ago. As I watched, Lavender's casket was unexpectedly lifted from the ground below and placed in my arms to cradle while the ground was prepared for them to be placed together.

In a remarkable turn of events, a blessing took place. When I was handed my baby daughter's casket in my arms decades after she left her short life for heaven, my heart swelled with love, and I could strongly feel her presence with me, along with my two living children, my son, and daughter, Crystal, who were right beside me in support.

This surreal moment was the only time I was ever together in this life with my three children. And it was profound. Within a few moments, several members of our family came close and placed their hands on the little pink casket holding the remains of my baby daughter.

It was especially poignant because my nieces and nephews, who were teens and young adults, may not have even been aware of Lavender's birth or death, and it was beautiful to see their respect and compassion given freely. As I write this, I am still in awe of the way my two children held me up as we treasured their sister, who left so long ago but remains in our consciousness and life forever, and for this, I am truly grateful.

Beauty in the Bittersweet: Crystal

As a child, she was an empath. She could feel people's emotions, give of her time and energy selflessly, and bring a playful lightness to even the darkest situations.

Dear Crystal, your bright light still rings true for me, as you are now. You are my greatest teacher and have always been so. Your experiences have taught me invaluable lessons in life. Many I resisted learning at the time because they were so painful. Even though I was given the opportunity to choose your day of birth in a planned cesarean delivery, I couldn't possibly imagine your life would end so suddenly as a young woman. On the last day that we were together on earth, it was your birthday. It was a beautiful lunch celebration overlooking the sea, with our young grandson joining in the celebration. If I had known it would be the last time we would see you alive on earth, I would have hugged you tighter and never let go of your hand. I miss you beyond comprehension. Life is so quiet without you in it. I miss your big smile and your big heart. I miss your laughter, your sense of humor, and the way you had an intuition about people and things going on around you. Your kindness and empathy were off the charts, and my life is blessed to have you still with me, sending messages and signs from the afterlife that keep us connected and united in love.

A few months after Crystal's passing, I experienced another poignant, surreal, and painfully beautiful moment with the spirit world supporting me, and this time, it was a one-and-only visit to the site of her death. At the time, it felt as if I was experiencing it in a dual reality as a grieving mother deep in sorrow, yet also as a soul able to observe it from above my body.

The morning before I arrived, I was so nervous and concerned about my emotional stability and strength in facing the reality, which I hoped would never come, that I almost canceled the visit. My husband knew it was something I had to do, yet our son, my only living child, was concerned about my well-being and questioned my reasons for going alone. I was to meet my daughter's close friend, and she would be there to greet me.

"It will be good for you," she stated.

I couldn't possibly understand how that could be true, but I moved forward, longing to feel closer to Crystal and to have the opportunity to honor her in this way.

As I left home, I took with me a shell-encrusted candle, a bouquet of silk flowers wrapped in pink ribbon, and a turquoise tag with my tearfully handwritten message: "For Crystal, Always Loved, Cherished, and Missed." Love, Mom.

When I arrived at the home, her friend was waiting outside to meet me for the first time. She invited me inside to see where my daughter had been living and handed me an olive-green canvas satchel that belonged to my daughter, containing the only belongings in this world she left behind. She had purchased it two days prior, and it was filled to the brim with greeting cards from her recent birthday, along with a few personal items. I clutched it to my heart and held my breath as I walked outside and down a path to the side of the house, where I was left alone.

As I looked down, I observed the rocky ground below where my daughter had died unnoticed in the dark of night. Someone had placed a rock with a cross painted on it, several vases of flowers, and an angel plaque stating, "Look for angels in your life. They are everywhere."

As I knelt, a white cat lingered nearby. I placed my hand on the ground, and my already broken heart cracked even further, if that was possible. Gently, I placed my gifts at the exact location where my bright and bubbly daughter had taken her last breath. My mind struggled to grasp this situation and what led to it, hoping with all my heart that she did not suffer. My spiritual belief caused me to imagine that one's soul painlessly leaves one's body quickly at the time of death and watches over the scene, much like I was doing at that moment. I imagined the freedom she must feel by being released from the burdens of addiction, and I could feel her presence alongside me, providing a comforting hug and an infusion of strength and resilience to carry me forward.

I chose at that moment to remember her as vibrant, happy, and smiling as her best self, and that vision continues to be in my mind's eye, meditations, and nighttime dreams. I kissed my hand and placed that kiss on the ground, leaving this place with a knowing that my daughter's spirit will always be with me.

Back in my car, I drove a short distance to sit by the ocean she loved, where we later celebrated her life and hugged her perfume-scented satchel to my heart with a feeling of gratitude for the essence of my sentimental daughter holding me up as I wept. I placed her red bandana on my cheek, and it brought tears to my eyes. I held the silver palm tree key chain, which had just one key, and wondered what door it would open. I reminisced in my mind about her generous nature, lighthearted exuberance, and sentimentality, and I continue to call on these qualities of personality in tribute to her.

Not a day goes by without recognition of her presence through awe-inspiring, soulful, inspired adventures in magical ways. I hear her words in the stillness of the night and in the light of the day, comforting and encouraging my journey through life, loss, and inspiration to share our story with you.

A few years later, I had the opportunity to reflect on this poignant day when I experienced a session of soul retrieval with a medium from my spiritual development circle, where I was able to revisit in meditation this location of my daughter's passing for greater healing. Before that session, just the thought or memory of that location held the emotional trauma of great loss. In the process of this session, I imagined myself visiting this site only instead of just leaving gifts on the rocky ground in memory of my daughter. This time, I was also given gifts to take with me on my grief journey.

In meditation, I left a large bright blue butterfly, a symbol of a connection with my daughter, dating back to her childhood. I had been drawn to butterflies in memory of Lavender after she provided the symbol of a lavender blue one as a sign from her. As a child, Crystal and I shared that connection.

Upon doing so, I felt blessed I was able to call back to my soul the fragments that had been left there on that sad day, and this time, I felt even more wrapped in love and compassion with a bit more acceptance rather than resistance to this great loss. I felt freedom where there was tension, and light streamed into the dark areas I carried within.

My daughters in spirit placed within my heart and soul a freshness like a burst of butterfly's light and free and a message to take with me on my grief journey. *Let there be joy within my being. Let there be patience, kindness, and love surrounding me.*

My dear, beautiful daughter Crystal,

Thank you for this opportunity to visit your site of passing once again, but to do so in peace, healing, and restoration. I am no longer fearful of going to that place in my mind. I am blessed to take away with me a golden angel statue and a blue rosary, both blessed by the angels above. Thank you for taking away my fear and for filling my heart with a freshness that felt like a burst of butterflies from my chest. Thank you for the release of pressure, giving relief like steam escaping a pressurized valve. The positive energy is flushing out the stagnant energy of pain and grief. There is freedom where there is tension. There is acceptance where there is resistance. I am able to welcome this peacefulness and smile.

The Places We've Gone

Of all the difficult places I've gone with you
This is uncharted yet familiar territory
as your older sister prepared me through the years
of keeping in contact with the other side.
Let this new journey together be beautiful.
I love you in heart and soul.

Eleven
Angels in Our Midst

"Everywhere you go, you have a team of angels, guides, and loved ones supporting, protecting, and encouraging you each step of the way. Being grateful for this universal presence is undoubtedly felt and multiplied within you."

—*Nancy Yuskaitis, Soulful Starlights*

Your guardian angels have been with you all your life and do a heroic job of protecting, guiding, comforting, and encouraging you from early childhood as you grew into a young adult, through mid-life, then into your later years and beyond as you learn about life, love, parenting, marriage, loss and letting go as well as compassion, forgiveness, and being a light to others.

Your guardian angel knows all about you, your passions, pursuits, faults, and failures, all that you have experienced and survived, as well as the healing transformation and soulful advances you've made along the way. He or she guides you and blesses you in protection, love, and light all the days of your life. It is their immediate response you can count on when called upon to assist you in every area of your life.

We each have one, two, or more guardian angels standing by our side. They may appear male or female, and their light is pure and bright. These loving beings are honored to walk this life's journey with us, night and day.

To your guardian angel, you are most important. You are their person. They do not have their own agenda, emotions, or dramas to contend with. Their only goal is to ensure your well-being and that of your soul. In the following pages, I hope to help you recognize your own guardian angel and the immense peace, calm, healing, and joy that knowing them can bring to your grief journey and life.

To fully appreciate their presence in your life, you only need to listen to your intuition to hear them, to open your heart to feel them, and to ask for their assistance to feel their blessings. Once you have felt or visualized your guardian angel in meditation, dreams, or journaling, allow yourself to feel the nurturing love being sent to you. Let this love take away your fears, your trauma, and your grief.

Ask your guardian angel to assist in releasing the heaviness, sadness, and deep loss within your energy system. Allow your angel to lighten your body, mind, spirit, and soul with a freshness of release and a feeling of safety, protection, pure lightness, and the return of joy.

Your guardian angel is available to you anytime. You can talk to them and ask them to come close to assist you, and you can be assured they will respond immediately. Ask your angel to fill the emptiness in your grieving heart with nurturing love, and let them encourage you to remember to practice self-love and self-care with the utmost compassion.

As I became familiar with my guardian angels through meditation and journaling, I became aware that there were two angels, one on either side of me with a hand on my shoulder supporting me through these hard life lessons of grief. On my left stands a beautiful female angel with soft, fluffy, heavily textured pink wings who has played many roles in my life. During times of deep grieving, she helps to nurture me in her warm embrace and to open my heart chakra again and again as it instinctively closes in pain and protection. She asked me to call her by the name of "Giovana," and her essence emits a pink rose fragrance that is familiar and healing to me.

She comforts me when I am hurting, struggling, or in the throes of grief. She also guides my process in helping others to heal, in afterlife communications, and in soul coaching. She provides more motherly energy than my own mother was able to provide to me. She also helps me to rise to meet challenges, including the loss of my two daughters, whom she has relationships with that are nurturing. Her protection has helped me through situations I encountered with opportunities for safety and grace. She works alongside a male angel who stands to my right with large blue wings and offers protection, uplifting reassurance, and blessings in every area of my life.

He is strong, skilled, and competent in areas of health, wellness, mediumship, grief recovery, creativity, forgiveness, and even tech support, and he asks to be called "Gabriel." In his gentle yet powerful way, he offers strength, confidence, and compassion when I feel weary. He also orchestrates assistance from the other spirit guides in my world, and he supports my drive to be an inspiration to others who have children or other loved ones in heaven and to oversee the soulful communications between us.

Just as mine are, your guardian angels are dedicated to you, your health, and your well-being. They are part of your personal spiritual guidance team from the afterlife to assist you in healing and foster uplifting ways to live and be of service. One day, I asked one of my guardian angels to introduce me to an angel of a family member, and soon, I could feel the presence of a male angel with bright blue textured wings. He was strong and resilient and was familiar with the energy in my soul family. His wings were hardy, having been through a lot with the ability to rise above difficult circumstances. He tells me his wings are strong like Teflon, durable, resilient, and beautifully capable of adding color, light, and softness to any situation. I asked him to please uplift someone in my family to feel the fullness of their being, strong, dynamic, and healthy, to feel love, joy, and healing in their heart. I then let it go and trusted in his efforts to assist.

Angel Message, for You

We ask that you be empowered with love, healing, and bravery to step out of your cocoon and let the world see you as you embrace the strength and resilience that is available to you. The earth is at a pivotal point, and all who choose to be open to the wisdom of the universe will benefit in immeasurable ways.

Twelve
Support Is Always Available

"Love and life continue on in unison, on different planes and different soul paths, while still being connected to our soul family."

—**Nancy Yuskaitis, Soulful Starlights**

I am deeply aware that my guardian angels provided immense healing to my being to comfort and support after the sudden loss of Crystal, as did my entire spiritual guidance team, and I am certain yours can provide whatever healing you may need in your life. You may or may not be familiar that, along with your guardian angels, you have others in spirit who love, encourage you, and walk with you in your grief.

These other angels and guides are aware of your thoughts, emotions, and experiences and realize how dreadful it is to lose a child or loved one, and they may hold your hand as they venture forward with you in your grief and healing. Each spirit guide alongside you has a special role, and each is helpful in assisting you to fulfill your purpose of healing and growth. There may be one master guide or soul guide who works with all the other angels and guides in overseeing your life, and there may be one or more that assist in many areas, such as family life, relationships, your wellness and healing, creativity and self-expression, etc. We each can learn to tune into our souls and to access the guidance and support from our own spiritual team in heaven.

Whether you are dealing with a health issue, a relationship disharmony, a transition in work, living arrangements, or a broken heart due to loss, you need to look no further than your own heart and soul. Call upon your angels and guides to walk with you and to assist you in healing your own life, body, mind, and heart, as well as assist and protect your loved ones and people and places around the universe.

You may be surprised and delighted to realize that you have a guide available for every area of your life, and some of these have been with you since birth or before and will remain with you.

There are "grief guides" who assist with grief support and recovery and provide healing for your pain and suffering following loss.

There are "intuition guides" who assist in strengthening and protecting your intuitive abilities and work with your energy to increase afterlife communication without it being draining and to facilitate opening your channel and closing it at the proper time.

There are "expression guides" who encourage thoughtful expression, decrease fear, and offer opportunities with the awareness of self-expression.

There is a "teaching guide" that provides pertinent development for soul growth.

A "health and medicine guide" assists with diagnosing imbalances, issues, or concerns, and clearing trauma and unnecessary stored emotions to foster greater well-being.

A "bodyworker guide" assists in releasing pain, blocked energy, tight muscles, grief, and trauma associated with loss and stressful situations.

There are "prosperity guides" to assist in protecting finances, investments, and assets and in attracting abundance with grace and ease.

"Relationship guides" assist in healthy friendships, marriage, and family ties.

"Creativity guides" can be for specific projects, such as writing this book or any art and design encouragement you may desire.

Your personal spiritual guidance team in the afterlife is filled with creative souls, joy bringers, and healers who inhabit your world in colorful ways to lighten and brighten your life. They bring energy and passion to assist you in healing your heart, softening your grief, and fostering endeavors that are uplifting to your soul. By opening yourselves up to connecting with your guidance team, you also open yourself up to a deeper level of soul work than you may have previously experienced.

Throughout these years of grief, I have been reminded time after time that my channel to spirit has been cleared and is open again, that the heavy denseness of grief can overshadow our creativity, energy, and ability to receive messages and signs from the spirit world and clearing is often necessary.

Affirmation: I can open and close this portal and open and close the golden door in the spirit realm and can turn up or down the golden light flowing between the two.

Once you have felt or visualized your own guardian angel or spirit guides in your life, let yourself accept the nurturing love that can take away your fear and trauma and lighten your grief. Ask your angel or guide to assist you in releasing the heaviness, sadness, and deep loss within your energy system. As this occurs, allow your body, mind, and spirit to breathe in a feeling of safety, protection, and joy. Let this nurturing love guide you in practicing soulful self-care and self-love.

RADIANCE is a master "soul guide" who radiates love, light, and gentleness. She is a believer in self-love, self-compassion, and kindness to ourselves, especially when we are hurting. She partners with my Jovial writing team in encouraging me to believe in myself and my abilities in this work of writing and to shine in all I do. She has been with me for a long time, through sad times and soulful ones, through joy and despair, illness and health, and through all the chapters of my life.

She is my "writing partner" for this book about sharing hope and love along with mystical, magical, mindful moments and messages from the afterlife. She ushers in my two daughters, with whom she is also connected, reminding me that I have much to learn from my Soulful Starlights, who have always expressed a purpose and passion for uplifting others. She has lived lives on earth and brings with her an understanding of the challenges and lessons of child loss and heartbreak, as well as rebirth and renewal. She embodies generosity of spirit and willingness to serve as she takes my hand, and we walk together in accomplishing our goals. She wears a pink heart in the center of her heart, and she gives me the gift of a gold heart surrounded by pink light to infuse my heart with love, light, and creative passion.

One of my guides, JEREMIAH, is a very large entity intent on protecting my energy. He literally picks me up when I'm feeling down and shakes the energy around me so that I can breathe in a more expansive manner. Whenever I feel myself slipping into the darkness or being weighed down by the heaviness of grief, all I need to do is ask him to step in and clear the energetic quality within and around me toward one of calmness and positivity in my home, marriage, family, and life. His influence has provided guidance to help me rise above difficult circumstances, enabling me to offer healing support and serve others through soul coaching and the creative arts.

YAK, a "mediumship guide," works alongside me to bring forward and guide souls from the spirit world to communicate more easily, and he supports me in standing in my intuitive power with confidence, conviction, and courage to be bolder in my approach. He is a translator of sorts, allowing the connection to be smooth and the messages to be what's needed.

A healing spirit guide, URSLA is also protecting my physical and emotional bodies as a Reiki guide. She balances my chakras and emotions, increases my energy, clears the channel for spirit communication, brightens my spirit, and cleanses my aura when my grief feels heavy. She also assists in my Reiki energy work in being a lightworker.

CHERISH, an angel who specializes in love, empathy, friendships, passion, and outreach, comes forward. Dressed in soft pink, she is open-hearted and open-minded. Her healing compassion is immense as she comforts those who ask for her assistance for balanced and loving relationships and for a way to provide loving self-care.

BLUE IRIS is an animal spirit guide in green and purple who radiates the energy of good health. She carries a pitcher filled with a magical potion of nurturing tea to dispel any imbalance and clear any blocks to perfect health and harmony.

ROSEBUD is a spirit guide for the emotional state of mind. She carries a pink rose she uses as a wand to dispel heavy energy with a light twist of the wrist, serving up moments of joy, hope, and lighthearted adventures.

DONAVON is a spirit guide for my passions and pursuits who has a knack for turning seemingly simple ideas into something meaningful. His guidance is bold, bright, and colorful. He is an artist for the soul and sets his sights on sharing creativity with the world.

KENDRA, a spirit guide for the spiritual body, can take one on a journey to the higher realms of possibility. She can be called on to usher in spirits for communication in my work and in healing bereaved souls.

JONQUIL, an angel, has been with me for about ten years and provides Soulful Inspired Adventures that bring lightness and joy to the experience. She works with me in all aspects of my daily life to discover and fulfill my purpose with the tools to express it. Her messages are of love, living with an open heart, staying true to the desires of your heart, and letting love flow through you, around you, above and below you, and expand out into the universe.

ROMAN helps to balance and strengthen loving relationships, and he can calm a situation and offer upliftment to encourage understanding. I call on him for his assistance to help keep my marriage loving, kind, and happy through all the challenges we've endured as a family.

Angel Healing

In a meditative healing session one day, I visualized myself resting in a treatment room in which there was an angel standing on each side of the door, waving me forward with gigantic feathers. I lay down on a comfortable platform table draped in white sheets. One angel had a blue heart on her chest, and the other a purple one. As several spirit guides entered the room chanting, I drifted off deeper and deeper into relaxation. Energetic light began to circle around the table in waves from the ground, lifting me off the table a few inches. Feeling weightless, I could see beams of light surrounding me, raising my vibration to a level higher than I could reach on my own with meditation. My mind was cleared of any discomforting thoughts to one of openness. My heart began to radiate within my chest in a heart shape of glowing amber light, healing, releasing, and cleansing my emotional body to the fullness of love. My root chakra was addressed next in an oval-shaped light that swirled around my body and presented the awareness of letting go of my desire to have things a certain way. Throughout the process, trusting in the how-to's and releasing attempts to control allowed my energy to flow lighter, free-er, and more joyfully.

I was asked to be less serious and to do everyday things with a lighter touch. *Let your gentleness out, release the constricted emotions and clenched intensity that your body holds from handling a great amount of pain and loss.*

Allow yourself to feel freer than you ever have. You have achieved a major transformation of healing in the years since Crystal's passing, but there is still unhealed pain you are holding onto. Let it go. Let it flow from your body to the earth in raindrops. Cry if you need to, sing, dance, move your body, and find healthy ways to let go. Shake your arms as if throwing off the weights holding you down from feeling weightless and free. You are a true warrior of strength and a powerful light. Let your heartache out, and let it radiate and shine more vividly. Release the constraints you feel to be a certain way. Be true to yourself. You are a perfect being of light and a beautiful soul of love.

Thirteen

Your Spiritual Guidance Team

"The love that bonds us is stronger than the grief that separates us."

—***Nancy Yuskaitis***

Your personal spiritual team in heaven is willing and waiting to be of assistance to you when called upon. *You are being asked to consider all your resources from angels, spirit guides, and loved ones on the other side, as well as your family, friends, and any support systems you may have in place in this life to help you heal.*

As you meditate or pray, expand your outreach to include all the people who honor your feelings and allow them to be expressed, and then move through you. Immense love is being sent to you with healing properties to assist your heart to stay open as you strive to heal.

If you are new to meditation, don't be concerned. It's a very simple process to learn. Begin slowly and for shorter times, even five minutes. Gradually allow yourself to meditate for longer sessions as it feels right to you. Ideally, twenty minutes is a perfect goal.

You are being asked to:
- Feel the love that resides within you; let it expand.
- Feel the creativity within your soul; let it flow.
- Feel the uplifting, radiant health that resides within.
- Let it grow throughout your body and soul.

A Spirit Message, for You

Whether you are dealing with a health issue, relationship disharmony, a transition in the home or work life, or a broken heart, you only need to look to your supportive angels and guides to assist you. There is a team willing and waiting to be of guidance, help, or to bestow blessings on those who request divine intervention. They are filled with such compassion for earth-bound souls, especially the ones who have lived a lifetime or two on the earthly plane.

There is much watching and waiting in the wings to be asked for assistance from those in need. You will never have to go through this pain alone. Your guidance team is available to lift you up and to give you a cause to celebrate life. LIVE LOVE CELEBRATE ... there is always something to celebrate in life. There is so much grace around you, prompting, inspiring, providing, allowing, and sharing. Be aware of all the blessings in your life and the goodness. The more you appreciate it, notice it, and have gratitude for it, the more it will follow. It is the law of attraction in action.

Let yourself be moved by laughter. Let it bring joy to your life. Let the joy overshadow the sadness. Let the love and joy get so big in your awareness that there is little room left for sadness. And when the sadness does come, and it will, especially on your late loved one's birthdays and anniversaries, let it circle around until you recognize it for what it is and then send it on its way. Imagine a spiral of color with dark to light. Let it swirl freely; notice it. Observe that the light area is much larger than the dark areas.

Let the dark area be lightened up by the lighter areas of your emotions. Let the darkness become looser and softer. Let the darkness be filled with light and fresh air. Let it breathe. As it does this, let it dissipate into the universe, leaving only lightness and vibrant color remaining. You can practice this anywhere, but it is preferable to be outside. Try it both ways while meditating inside and outdoors. You will be amazed at the improved well-being you will feel.

It is a very gentle process to meet and become acquainted with your spirit guides, whose energy and presence can feel familiar to you once you become aware of their presence in your life. We each have a main soul guide from life to life given by God. In meditation, you can request to have them come forward to meet with you. They can provide details to you about yourself in this life and other lives before this one. My principal soul guide is "OTIS," a messenger of goodwill with long silver hair who wears a pale purple gown. He has partnered with me throughout the ages in a calm, reassuring, wise, and generous manner. In meditation during our first meeting, he shared with me that he has cared for me with grace and protection for my ultimate well-being, even though we've never personally met in meditation or life before this time.

He states that he is an overseer of my life plan and has sent many spirit guides to assist and lift my spirits. "Every life is fraught with challenges, but in this life, you have been brought to the brink of your ability to cope with situations from childhood to the present, and that is where your guides can step in to carry you forward. Each lesson, each hardship, and each loss has propelled you into a pillar of strength with gentleness, grace, generosity, and a heart full of compassion with an innate ability to love and receive love. This love is universal and available to everyone. It is a love fragrant with the sweetness of a flowering gardenia, soft as a rose petal, and lovely as a seashell. It swirls around in shades of pink and white, healing any areas of painful emotions, softening the edges to bring a calmness to your being and to others."

You are mastering all that has challenged you, dear one.

In this first meeting, I was given my soul name, "Roselle," meaning compassionate and kind. I am told that in other lives, I also suffered great loss and became bitter, but in this lifetime, I have accepted healing from the angelic world in order to stay compassionate and kind. I am also reminded that my longtime marriage has given my soul the love, security, and genuine care it deserves, offering me immense healing and growth. My transcendence over the heartache I've experienced in many areas has provided me with knowledge, experience, and the gift of speaking my truth as I guide others in living consciously.

Seek the Light

"When darkness comes, and it will grasp hold of the light,
Let it illuminate your world.
When you desire to feel close to me, let nature be your guide,
Soak in the awe-inspiring beauty and let it shine upon you as you grieve.
You are loved. You are guided. You are not alone.
Peace be with you."

*—**Soulful Starlights***

Fourteen

Jovial Angels, Spirit Guides, & Muses

"Embrace the love and beauty in your life. Even in difficult times, it can soothe your soul."

—*Nancy Yuskaitis*

We are artists, adventurers, joy makers, intuitives, and love bearers. *We are your Jovials. We are the joy bringers, the creative souls that inhabit your world in all the colorful ways that lighten and brighten your world. We bring energy and passion to you to develop new ways to share your love, light, and healing with the world. We encourage laughter, joy, and soulful-inspired adventures. We are also your writing muses.*

Passionate Ones, let your spirit sing. Let your heart be saturated with abundant love. We ask that the readers of this book be empowered with love, healing, and bravery to step out of their self-imposed cocoon and let the world see their beauty and light as radiant and free.

About ten years ago, I was introduced to the Jovials, which is led by SOULFUL SAM, a spirit guide who states *whether we realize it or not, the health and well-being of our soul play a big role in how the events of our life are lived out. Taking special care of our soul is vital as we grow through our life's lessons while being mindful of self-care and self-love.*

His energy is very similar to my maternal grandfather, gentle and soft-spoken. As the head guide in my Jovial team, he requests the assistance of other guides to come forward at differing times in my life, calling for different assistance. He is one of my biggest fans and understands how dreadful it is to grieve the loss of a child as he walks the path of grief hand-in-hand with me, offering comfort and support. While writing this book, I became aware that my grandfather, Sam, had indeed lost a baby girl after my mom was born, yet no one ever mentioned it to me, and I believe my paternal grandparents also lost a child as an infant that no one spoke of again.

Keeping child loss private in my world stops here as I am boldly and bravely sharing the life and loss of my two beautiful daughters as part of my legacy with the intention to comfort and assist others grieving the loss of a loved one.

My JOVIAL team consists of IRIS, a "young female spirit guide" who says purple is her color, and she assists in spiritual life coaching in mindfulness, meditation, and marketing.

JOURNALISM JOE, a spirit guide and writing coach, assists with ideas for this book and other writing projects.

GEORGE is a master spirit guide who oversees newly departed souls with whom I may have contact in my mediumship. He is part of an immense team working alongside souls who pass suddenly. As these souls are dazed and confused at first, his team assists in their adjustment, giving them great relief as they prepare for their life review.

These souls are directed to reflect in a way that provides contrast to their life experiences. Many express the emotions of regret for having been unable or unwilling to forgive others who offended them in their life. Some are filled with regret at the loss of joy they experienced. His team offers these souls a light that permeates through their fear, anxiety, blocks, and walls, awakening their consciousness and heart.

SANYA, a Hawaiian sage, works to clear ancestral energy that is not beneficial to my well-being. Her long, dark hair glistens with silver. She instructs that I am to share with my readers the guidance to teach them how to walk lightly on this earth in peace, grace, and in the comfort of the heart. Grief does not need to be carried so heavily as time passes, once one learns to live with lightness of heart.

Jovial Suggestion

As you sit or lie down quietly, focus on your breathing as you inhale and exhale slowly a few times.

Invite a familiar soul in spirit to join you and share in this experience. Ask for a spirit guide to assist you in connecting with the higher dimensions of the afterlife in search of answers to questions you may have.

Questions to ask yourself:

How can you?

- Breathe Fresh Air into Your Soul
- Uplift Your Soul
- Offer Healing to Your Soul
- Be Kind to Your Soul
- Nurture Your Soul
- Listen to Your Soul

Soulful Notes

_____
_____
_____
_____
_____
_____
_____
_____
_____
_____
_____

The Jovial Team encourages transformation, resiliency, and taking chances on experiencing joy again after confirmation of life after life.

You may have other beings of light join you, like PENELOPE, who in mediation one day, handed me a purple tablet like a scroll and a gold pen with a white feather on the cap to take notes to share with you. Opening yourselves up to connecting with your guidance team also opens you up to a deeper level of soul work than you may have previously experienced.

Soulful Suggestion

Begin a meditation and ask that one of your guardian angels or spirit guides join you in facilitating an adventure with a loved one in spirit. It can be to experience doing something they loved in life or something you enjoyed sharing together. It could be cooking, gardening, hiking, fishing, or anything that sparked joy in your loved one's life and would light up your being now. Ask that this be a beautiful healing experience for you both, blending your worlds and creating a time and space to communicate what they loved about their life and what they hope you can learn from this experience. This exercise can offer the opportunity to propel you with a renewed purpose and passion to start something new, proceed with a current project, or receive the impetus to complete it. What can you fulfill in honor of your loved one at this time? Ask for any insights on family matters that could benefit from some assistance in facilitating greater healing and allowing more joy into your life.

SECTION 3

Grief Journey

"Grief sets you in a mode of survival, and your world becomes very narrow. Self-preservation is necessary at this fragile time to build up your strength and resiliency."

—*Nancy Yuskaitis*

Grief has been a major life lesson for me in this lifetime and has provided the opportunity to become emotionally strong, soulfully resilient, calm in the midst of chaos, forgiving and resistant to holding grudges, expressive in creative and inspired ways, heartfelt and kind, able to speak my truth and to be a mother who cares deeply for her children, stands up for them, is present and available and who leads by example in heart-centered conscious living, but it didn't happen overnight.

In the immediate heartbreak of child loss for the second time, I struggled with my will to go on living as the darkness of grief sought to overwhelm me. Every day, it took immense effort to sit with my grief, feel my emotions, and look for a spark of hope to lift the heavy weight of sadness. I began each day with thoughts of what one does when they are overcome with the emotions of a reality they cannot change. In my heart, I wanted to stay in this place and grieve, but as I felt myself slipping away to a dark and uncomfortable place, I chose to fight hard, gather all my energy, and allow myself to be uplifted by the encouragement I received from my two daughters in spirit to guide my way to a more hopeful, peaceful and loving space to grieve.

Grief is as unique as the person experiencing it. Your emotions can take you on a roller coaster ride where you may find exhilaration and then despair, excitement and then fear, joy and then sadness, and this may occur repeatedly throughout your life. However, through it all, your soul remains intact. We each can feel the way we do in any given situation and make adjustments that benefit our well-being.

After experiencing loss, our heart can shut down in protective self-defense, and numbness can set in, dulling the pain somewhat but also dulling any attempt to experience feelings of hope, gratitude, or joy. Once your heart has been emotionally cracked open, it can feel as if parts of it are truly missing. It may seem as if they have been ripped out and taken with our loved ones, leaving us to live forever with broken hearts. It becomes imperative to discover ways to relieve the pain of heartbreak, soothe your heart and soul, and feel comforted in the belief that the love between you and your loved one still exists. Within the experience of grief is compassion for ourselves and other grieving souls.

Fifteen
Life after Child Loss

"To My Daughters: My heart, I give you along with my love and my promise as your mother to feel your presence with me always."

—*Nancy Yuskaitis*

Grief has existed within my heart for my entire adult life. Grief has been my constant companion and has walked with me every step of the way. Grief has taught me to be tender and kind to myself and to look for ways to feel nurtured in everyday experiences. The sun upon my skin, the sweet scent of a rose, the words of a song, the sight of the ocean, a warm embrace, a tender touch, a sign from spirit, and the love and kindness of friendship each have a way of improving my sense of well-being.

My grief is a feminine energy filled with empathy, love, and immense compassion. She, like me, is filled with a sense of wonder and gratitude at the comfort received by believing that life exists beyond one's passing and that our loved ones are happy, healthy, and always available to offer love and support to us from heaven in awe-inspiring ways.

Yet living through child loss is like being acutely aware of every minute of the day and night as you are experiencing it until sleep overcomes you in welcome respite. Every tear is felt emotionally and physically, your attention span is short, and every minute distraction is painfully noticed. Leaving the house exposes your vulnerability and raw emotions, and when arriving back home, there is grief to greet you so strongly. It affects every fiber of you.

Some days, chills would come over my body, and weakness would descend, causing me to sit down, but after a while of resting, meditating, or calming and centering myself, I would rise with a rush of intention to keep going in my marriage, home, garden, writing, and life as I sought to experience a sense of relief from the crushing pain.

DEAR CRYSTAL, my life changed forever the day you left. My heart shattered into a million little pieces, and my soul ached for you. I don't know who I am without you. The highs, the lows, new beginnings of hope and promise, second chances, renewal, and childlike enthusiasm filled my life, along with your tenacity, resiliency, boundless energy, and selfless giving. My heart, I give you my love and my promise as your mother to feel your presence with me always.

I've had so much loss in my life, and yet nothing compares to the depth of my sorrow in the loss of you. My mind cannot grasp the reality of this loss, yet the emptiness inside tells me differently. My entire body weeps in non-stop tears, chest pain, and chills. I can barely hold my head upright to sit here and write. Sleep is the only true relief from this suffering, as it feels as if the air has been let out of my life. I pray for peace, acceptance, strength, and comfort to survive and thrive in what's left of my beautiful life. Love, always. ~ Mom

It is a harsh reality to acknowledge the dreadful fact that her bubbly personality will no longer walk in that door or enliven the kitchen with her culinary skills and desire to please. My life feels incredibly empty because she's not here.

I choose to make a conscious decision to guide my emotions back to a neutral state, where I immediately feel a wave of safety come over me as I rest. It is the type of presence of mind that occurs when all is well in your world. When your children are safe in the protective cocoon of your home, where everyone is accounted for, you can relax your worrisome mothering mind and bask in the comfort that your baby is safe.

Having just arrived home from a visit with our son and his wife, I observed that familiar feeling of being close to him. It startled me to realize I was experiencing that level of peace with Crystal, yet I was. Her spirit in our home was so strong that she felt alive, right alongside me. Our emotional connection was intact, and the light and happy aspect of her personality was felt so strongly that I knew it was real. This is her world; she is at home in that little cottage by the sea where her body lives in a box on the shelf, but her spirit and soul live free.

I pondered motherhood with love as vast as the ocean, and in that sea, sometimes there are baffles that slow down the transmission of waves, and grief is like that, it comes in waves of love. At times, they are gentle, and at other times, crashing, yet the essence remains. Love is everlasting and transcends effortlessly between our two worlds.

Talk to me, I plead. I need you. I miss you. Please stay with me for a while. Life isn't the same without you.

How do you live without someone who is a part of you, who you feel so energetically tied to that you feel each other's pain and joy? It is a loss that never goes away. I live each day with a blanket of sadness draped over me, and some days, it's almost too heavy to carry, but I do.

8 months after: Returning home one day, as I walked through the front door of our seaside cottage in the Florida Keys, tears began to seep from my eyes in a flow I couldn't control. Immediately, I was aware of my daughter Crystal's presence with me. Just inside the entryway was our dining room, and our buffet was adorned with a display of mementos and treasures belonging to her, along with a turquoise blue box containing her ashes, nestled among shells and small photographs. I am aware that her spirit is everywhere, yet the sadness I felt was palpable. I placed my hands on the pretty blue box and greeted my daughter with all the love that was in my heart. It was a brief greeting, as the car waited to be unloaded, but an intentional one, a heart-wrenching one, as I learned to live alongside her in a new way.

12–15 months after: I find myself struggling with the emptiness that remains in my life. It is so deep that it cuts through my entire body, leaving a gaping hole of shredded emotions and heartache. The pain is so pervasive that it renders me listless while it saps my energy from under me. I clutch my aching chest and pray for healing to survive this physical and emotional pain. There is also gratitude and much to be grateful for in special moments with family and friends and the continued loving support of my spirit team, including my Soulful Starlights. The beauty and light shown to me are powerfully healing and uplifting in my sorrow.

15–24 months after: The heavy blanket of grief and sadness has lifted, and most days, there is a lightness in my spirit and step. I've learned to live with my two daughters' presence around me, and I can talk to them anytime. The longing remains, and so does the connection between mother and daughter, although they are the ones doing the nurturing.

As the seasons change, so do I. There is beauty in my life and gratitude for the blessings of which I'm acutely aware. There is still emptiness and pain from the loss of Crystal's physical absence, but miraculously, I feel her comfort me in my grief, fits of anger, and regret.

24 months: I acknowledge that I have not only survived, but I have grown through grief in ways that can be seen and felt and in ways that only my soul understands. There is light in my life again. My heart is open, and joy is free to visit on a frequent basis. My daughters are gone from this life, and they are still with me from their place in the afterlife. The peace this provides of their continued existence in my life experience is remarkable. The broken pieces of my heart have been tended with their love, compassion, and kindness. I celebrate how far I've come in my grief journey. I recognize my inner strength and embrace my mindful intentions with grace and gratitude. Taking the time to heal while discovering new ways to transform grief by breathing fresh air into the darkness through nature, creativity, and enjoyment in cherished relationships is soulful self-care in action.

Soulful Suggestion

I find it helpful to be conscious and aware of how I am relating to my experience of traumatic loss. As early as possible in your grief journey, I encourage you to begin writing down your emotions as they arise in a journal or other document. This will allow your grief to breathe as you free up the heavy emotions in self-expression. It is up to you whether you save these writings as I did or burn them as an expression of emotional release.

Live Each Day

When life seems impossible and the pain of loss too great
When going on seems unbearable and carrying on too heavy
When agony drains your energy, and the future looks bleak
When sadness overwhelms you and isolation leaves you lonely
Look to the stars for strength, and know you're not alone
I'm right here alongside you, offering peace, love, and comfort
as you grieve
Live each day for me, will you? In kindness, grace, and love
Let the beauty you see be my gift, lightening your sorrow
and your grief

Sixteen

Soulful Grief Reflections

"Each loss that we suffer of those we love makes life increasingly more soulful, heartfelt, and poignant."

—*Nancy Yuskaitis, Soulful Starlights*

My grief process has held a position front and center in my life for many years. No matter what I was doing after Crystal's passing, it included thoughts of her. Writing my grief reflections down became a way to express, address, and receive comfort in the moment through afterlife communication.

It provided the opportunity to bring awareness to these painful feelings and to infuse them with a breath of fresh air and light. I was then able to determine what was needed to provide a healing balm to my grieving heart. The following topics are ones that were lessons in understanding amid the heartbreak of loss.

Emotions

Grief is a transformational experience, and each of us navigates it differently at different times. One thing is for sure: it is filled with emotions that can overwhelm your life and your entire being, leaving you seeking relief from the crushing pain of a shattered heart repeatedly. As you strive to heal, it is essential to express yourself in ways that feel right to you.

Many times in our lives, grief can play a role in our emotions, which can affect every aspect of our lives. It may be the reality of the loss of a loved one, our health, livelihood, or other challenging life situations that we must learn to traverse. This grief is personal; it is ours alone, and it is unique to our personality, life, and relationships. The way we live with our grief varies from moment to moment depending on our emotional state of mind, mindset, personal philosophy, the empathy and compassion we receive from others, and whatever else we may discover that is helpful to calm our fears, soothe our soul, nurture our spirit, comfort our heart and live peacefully with our personal loss by our side.

At first, grief feels so large that it takes its place front and center in our lives. It affects our mood, energy level, and how we spend our time. It can even fluctuate from moment to moment, hour to hour, and day by day, depending on the level of our suffering at that time. Grief is an ever-evolving process as we re-adjust daily to a reality we didn't choose and discover ways to live within it that are comforting, uplifting, and encouraging.

Grief required my focused attention to begin opening my heart again. Loss can take an open, loving heart, and just as suddenly as loss can occur, the pain of immense grief can feel as if your heart was shattered into a million pieces that will never heal again. I am here to tell you that it will. It will never be the same as it was before your loss, but it can still be beautiful in its new form.

In my own experience, I came to realize that I felt the loss of each loved one differently, and to the understanding that we each respond to our experience in a way that feels appropriate to us. Many factors determine its differences, such as the type of relationship, whether the relationship was complicated, the type of passing that can be extremely traumatic, the level of closeness with the individual, and whether forgiveness is important on either side. In some situations, the cause of death is clear, and other times, we must accept that there are unknown circumstances surrounding it.

One thing is certain, there is no getting over the loss of a loved one. There is only learning to live with it tucked inside our hearts in the best way possible for our own healing and growth. I found it's essential to stay open-minded as you seek to feel your loved one's presence, and you may observe the signs that the spirit world sends you, offering a more peaceful way to live without their physical presence in your life.

In time, day by day, step by step, with awareness and intention, your big, beautiful heart can begin to soften its sharp edges and allow light to seep into the cracks, opening the closed parts and mending the broken ones. I embrace how far I have come in my grief journey. I recognize my inner strength and acknowledge my focus to make every day the best it can be with mindful intention, grace, gratitude, and a heart full of empathy and love for you. I have faith that you, too, are stronger than you ever thought was possible.

My Soulful Starlights brought the following guidance flowing into my awareness as I struggled with the effects of grief on my emotions.

Soulful Suggestion

Visualize how your state of mind contains lighter and darker emotions. Become aware of how the intensity of each emotion feels to you. Observe how the shades change and evolve as we do every day. When we accept our feelings and, without holding on too tightly, we let them drift freely through us, it can transform how we feel. If we hold onto even a portion of fear, anxiety, rejection, loss, or grief too tightly, it can cause unhappiness, imbalance, and at times illness. I encourage you to stay flexible as your emotions ebb and flow, lighter and darker, as they come close and fade away. You have control over your emotions, and honoring them and giving them the freedom to shift will bring uplifting opportunities for you to experience new feelings.

Solitary Grief

As you lie in the darkness of grief, you may feel a sense of contentment in your isolation that makes you want to pull away from the world around you and just stop and be alone.

It's self-protection, and although you often long for others to reach out with a comforting hand, a compassionate heart, and understanding, you do realize that this is your process. It was your child or loved one, and no one else feels the loss the way you do. The physical pain of heartbreak will wake you up each morning with anguish, sadness, and despair so heavy you can barely lift yourself out of bed. It can feel like cruel torture not to have the support of family or friends by your side in your darkest hours. However, by accepting the comfort and love from the spirit world to soothe, uplift, and support you through the sorrow, you can be restored by hope and love.

There were certain times when I felt overwhelmed with heartache, but I also felt it was compounded by the lack of empathy shown to me throughout my life. It took much soul-searching and many tearful bouts of expression as I gained insight into my heart, soul, thoughts, behavior, and attitude. I determined, through insights from the spirit world and inner guidance, that I must learn to accept the things I cannot change, to forgive myself and others, and to redirect my thoughts when they cause me increased heartache and suffering.

These were not new realizations, yet they were being shown to me so that I could see how it was keeping me from moving forward to experiencing more joy in my life. Along with addressing these unresolved emotions through conversation, meditation, spiritual coaching, soul retrieval, and journal writing, I found it helpful to write my intentions for healing and change in my journal as things progressed. I asked the spirit world for insight and assistance, and my Soulful Starlights responded with the following.

Grief can cause you to recoil in self-protection, and it can also leave you disappointed in the lack of support you receive from those closest to you, causing you to question your value in their lives. Know that your love is immense and your compassion unsurpassed. Although people close to you don't always show you that they care, they truly do. You matter, you are important, and you are valued for your presence in their lives. Be the strong soul that I know you are, and live your life without wondering if you are loved or appreciated. Just be who you are and express yourself in all the ways you do without expecting anything from others.

Release yourself from the emotions of lack that you experience at times of loneliness. Just keep focused on what you have to offer and not what you are missing. Shift your process and share value with the world. Be fiercely independent in your creativity and in your life. Let that hole in your heart that is missing love and nurturing be filled with strength, grit, and grace. You are one-of-a-kind, and you must learn to let yourself shine in all your beauty and expression. There is nothing to feel insecure or invisible about; be proud of yourself. You are smart, beautiful, and a wonderful human being with love, compassion, and gifts to share that, without question, will be important and valuable to this world.

Crystal shares how important it is to love and be loved without judgment, without fear, and to live with an open heart full of goodness and grace for all. She reminds me of the importance of sitting in the quiet stillness to listen to messages from the spirit world. As I struggled in my grief, desiring more support from others in my life, she reminded me.

Relationships come and go and are meant to last at varying times in our lives. Accepting the situation when family or friends stay distant is an opportunity to realize that not everyone sees beyond their immediate viewpoint. Live your life without emotional expectations from others and accept the freedom that comes from not having them, only to be let down. Keep your head looking forward, your heart open, your spirit brave and free. Give generously to those who desire your love, energy, or support in this wondrous life.

Soulful Suggestion

Release:
- Expectations of others' behavior toward me.
- Expectations of how things should be.
- Disappointment with how things are.
- Heartache over the way things are (out of my control).
- Longing for things to always be (unrealistically) different.
- Need to prove myself (as hurting, grieving, or as being okay).
- Feeling let down by loved ones in the present and in the past.

Discover:
- My own inner peace—joy—space to just be.
- Ways to uplift and reclaim joy.
- A relationship with my own soul.

Be:
- Grateful – Present – Calm – Content – Creative – Compassionate – Conscious
- Hopeful – Peaceful – Mindful – Thoughtful – Kind – Gracious – Forgiving
- Resilient – Happy – Purposeful – Intuitive – Adventurous – Resourceful
- Accepting What Is – True to Myself

Be:
- Less judgmental.
- Less reactive (triggered to feel bad).
- Less easily offended or hurt.

Do:
- Sparkle. Shine. Radiate. Light.
- Release. Relinquish. Rejoice.
- Check in with yourself each day.
- Read something inspiring.
- Write in your journal.
- Sit or walk in nature.
- Meditate.
- Practice self-care.
- Experience and enjoy soulful, inspired adventures.

Strive to:
- Accept people the way they are.
- Offer compassion, kindness, and love or at least neutral energy.
- Observe, heal, and release painful experiences in the past.
- Use my observer self to recognize my words, actions, and behavior.
- Release my need for things to be different.
- See the beauty, not the imperfection.
- Embrace but not embody tension.

Grief Attacks: Triggers—Grief Activators

Soulful Grief Reflections

Grief triggers can be mild, or they can take your breath away.

They can come and go quickly, or they can turn your day upside down.

They can leave you momentarily sad as your emotions of grief pass through you or can leave you brokenhearted and curled up on the floor in a puddle of tears.

It's completely weird how one can be going along in their day, working or taking care of necessary things and maybe even be experiencing a little joy again in their life when suddenly they are triggered by a memory, song, scent, photo, or just about anything, and it can totally throw them off balance. It can feel as if all the air has been let out of the room. Any pleasant feelings previously felt dissipate, leaving a heaviness and tightness in your chest, along with labored breathing. I am familiar with these experiences and have too often been blindsided by them, only to feel the comforting presence of my daughters to uplift and support my grieving process once again.

Island Lunch: 4/13/18

One spring day, my husband and I spontaneously decided to stop at a seafood restaurant in Stock Island for lunch. They are known for their delicious hogfish sandwiches, and we had enjoyed dining there with Crystal in the past. I had been feeling emotionally okay that day until we arrived in the parking lot, where I was caught off guard by an outpouring of emotions that were triggered by just being at that restaurant. By the time we were ready to be seated, the wave of grief had consumed me, causing tears to pour down my face, lasting the entire meal. The memories of being there with her were strong, as was her presence with us.

Mom, I couldn't resist being there with you two today. You were in my stomping grounds, and I wanted to share this experience with you. It was always a favorite place of mine, and I remember sharing it with you two. I am aware that sometimes my presence is felt so strongly that it brings an avalanche of tears. Good tears, the kind you have when sharing a heartfelt experience but, in this case, mingled with sadness. Love, always.

Anticipatory Grief

Bereaved Mother's Day is celebrated the Sunday before Mother's Day and is one of those occasions that can cause you to begin stressing and be tearful in advance of the approaching holidays. For those who have lost a child, children, and or their own mother, an array of emotions, including fear, can arise knowing your loved one won't be here to celebrate with you. On my first Mother's Day without Crystal, I was deep in the process, feeling every bit of emptiness, but as the day arrived, I also felt blessed to be surrounded by family, as it was also my husband's birthday that weekend. To acknowledge my daughters, I felt drawn to bring home two bouquets of roses that I knew they had helped me choose. I placed them in separate vases, symbolizing the love and presence of each with beauty and grace.

Usually, I have anticipatory grief for days leading up to a birthday or anniversary, my daughter's celebration of life anniversary, and the acknowledgment of infant loss day, International Wave of Light, Overdose Awareness Day, and other important days celebrated in memory.

Since I am aware my emotions may be fragile as these dates approach, I pay special attention to providing soulful self-care and giving myself an abundance of compassion and understanding.

Tears May Fall

From the Starlights... As your emotions live on the surface and tears come easily, let them come. Let yourself cry. Let the tears stream down your face. Let your emotions out, the ones that bubble to the surface, let them out. As the tears stop and the intense emotion you are feeling is released, allow a calmness to come over you, leaving you feeling lighter in sadness.

In times of grieving, it's important to be receptive to allowing light to wash over you and illuminate your life as you let your heart and spirit open slowly, bit by bit.

Throw off the heaviness and allow light to stream in and fill your heart with renewed hope and promise. As you walk through this day, I invite you to allow your heart to be lightened from any heaviness it carries from grief, trauma, and difficult life circumstances in your past or present.

Imagine that you are a light being filled with the potential to shine brightly in radiant joy and love. Take a moment to be mindful of lightening up, letting go, and bringing to your awareness the kind, loving, joyful soul that you are.

Breathe in the release and the joy. Let it swirl around your being, filling it with lightness and peace. You are radiant. As you acknowledge it, imagine a beautiful watering can that can be filled with love, light, and kindness in your hand. As often as possible, sprinkle radiant joy and kindness throughout your life with intention, gratitude, and grace.

Regret

Our relationship was always a dance tinged with a lot of emotion, partly due to a longing for each other to be different, yet we still offered unconditional support to each other. There was frustration and guilt on both sides in the last years of her life, with so many difficult starts and abrupt ends. I felt like a brightly colored balloon that was recharged each morning to face the day with hope and enthusiasm and the best of intentions for her, only to be deflated at day's end. She, too, would inflate with hope and promise, purpose and passion, only to deflate in drama and disappointment again. After her passing, I was overcome at times with regret for so many things, but most of all, our life journey on this earth together was over.

Anger

Anger can take many forms in your grief process; I know it has for me. It can vacillate between anger at yourself, at your loved one for pain caused in life and in their leaving, anger at whoever or whatever may have caused this loss, and anger at life itself. Sometimes, grievers are even mad at God. Anger may be combined with sadness and a feeling of being sick to your stomach that can't be fixed but can be reduced through compassion, understanding, and love. I'm being told that giving or receiving hugs from family and friends is helpful as they offer reassurance that you are not alone on this journey.

It is helpful to discover healthy ways to process and release this anger not to cause more harm or slow your healing progress. In my situation, Crystal was very attuned and attentive to my feelings and our experience from the afterlife, but not necessarily while she was living. She was insistent on reaching out to me to explain many things, and if I was distracted or consumed by grief, she would keep trying until she got through to express her apology.

1/16/17

Mom,

You know I have been trying to reach you. I know you are in another phase of your grief recovery, and I am here to help you. Don't try to go it alone. I can assist. I understand that you've felt anger in this next phase, and that is positive. It means you are moving along and not stuck in the process.

It's ok to be mad at me, at our dysfunctional relationship, and the crazy, stupid choices I made along the way that drove you crazy, but you stayed with me until it got too burdensome. I understand. I have so much to say that I regret not saying when I was there with you, but now I can tell you those things as I have a better understanding of life on earth.

Let me help you; don't turn away from me at this time. I know you feel distraught by losing me, and I want you to feel relief. It is your time to regain your energy and to live fully in the present while there is time. Don't spend too much time lamenting my pitiful life. I was ok with most of it, really. I'm just concerned that I hurt you so many times over years and years.

Let it go. Let yourself be freed of the turmoil I caused in your life. Let yourself be happy & carefree. Sit here and let me speak to you. I have much to say, and I am here for you. I love you, now and always.

Fear and Anxiety

After experiencing child loss as a very young mom and later in life, I can attest that fear has a role so large it needs to be managed, or it will overpower any peace of mind you have achieved. At first, fear shows up as panic and permeates your world, causing you to be fearful of something that causes you this much pain to occur again. Fear is such a part of grief that it keeps showing up to scare you again and again. There is fear surrounding your living children, grandchildren, spouse, siblings, or parents, and a deep desire with all your heart for them to stay safe and healthy. When there is stress, illness, or concern for our loved ones, the fear rises and causes us anxiety that may manifest in physical symptoms or emotional overwhelm.

When fear threatens your emotional well-being, I find it helpful to take a moment or twenty for myself, sit or lie down, and just breathe. Asking the spirit world to assist you in prayer to lessen your fear and remove the anxiety is worth approaching with the highest of intentions for the safety and protection of yourself and your loved ones.

Cumulative and Compounded Grief

Lavender's passing has helped me to glean wisdom to heal the present. Many decades had gone by, and many chapters had opened and closed in my life, when I found myself as a grieving mother for the second time. I was much older, wiser, and more prepared to self-nurture and receive unlimited support from family and the spirit realm, yet even with these resources, the loss of Crystal was felt so deeply that I soon realized I was being called to grieve both of my daughters at the same time.

Prior to Crystal's unexpected departure, I had been enjoying life with my husband and looking forward to a wonderful summer at our home in the high mountains of Crested Butte, Colorado. Receiving the call from my son to my husband, confirming that she was gone just about destroyed me. My heart was broken in unfathomable ways, and grief consumed my life.

As the days went by, I became aware that my emotional pain was not only felt for the loss of my grown daughter, but it was cumulative grief magnified tenfold in bringing up emotions from the loss of my infant daughter decades prior. The loss of a second child seemed unbelievable and hard to grasp in my suffering and inconsolable despair. I understood, though, that I must grieve the loss of both of my girls simultaneously as I could feel the presence of each of them in their united bond to support and comfort me from the afterlife.

When Lavender left for heaven, I hadn't personally known anyone who had ever lost a child. When Crystal went to join her sister, I didn't know anyone who had lost two children. I didn't know how I could possibly bear it, and yet I did. I'm here to encourage you that, with patience, love, and compassion for yourself, along with the support available to you in this life and from the afterlife, you can find new strength in believing that you can and will survive, knowing your children and loved ones are still by your side.

In your prayers for peace and relief, ask the spirit world to offer healing and support to you, both while you sleep and in every waking moment when you may need it. Be gentle with yourself. It's imperative. Try to implement some of the suggestions I've given you throughout this book to prioritize self-care and comfort you. Reach out and seek the support of a mental health professional, grief therapist or grief counselor, spiritual life coach, psychic medium, and additionally, a grief support group, online or in person.

Physical Aspects

There is no doubt that each of us experiences grief differently, although there are similarities in the physical reactions and symptoms within our bodies. It's important to seek medical care, especially if you have ongoing conditions that require managed care.

It's amazing how widespread the symptoms can be, including but not limited to tightness and heaviness in the chest, gastrointestinal issues, lack of energy and fatigue, sleep disturbance, muscle pain, shortness of breath, numbness and tingling, and headaches.

I highly encourage you to seek professional care in relieving, managing, or supporting your physical health in various ways.

My grief journey has included many of these symptoms in my early grief and again in the last year as I was writing this book. Sharing our story has been an immersive experience of soulful, emotional, and creative expression, yet it's like being in process all the time. It has taken the support of holistic and medical guidance as well as ongoing self-care to release the symptoms of grief that have been stirred up in my emotional and physical body.

May you receive the guidance and support you need from the spirit realm and from knowledgeable sources familiar with grief therapy in physical, emotional, and cognitive responses to loss.

Forgiveness

Apology and forgiveness are big topics, and many relationships can relate to it from spouses, former spouses, parents, siblings, and children who were left without being given the I'm sorry they hoped for while a loved one was living, so that forgiveness can begin.

In my own family, receiving an apology from my mother, my ex-husband, and my daughter, Crystal, all provided the opportunity to let go of unresolved emotions of hurt, resentment, or immense disappointment that clouded my memory of them after their passing. In the afterlife, our loved ones undergo a life review, during which they can see clearly how they may have hurt others in their life. They see it in living color, just how their behavior, attitude, and words affected others in hurtful, disregarding, or abusive ways. They are privy to an inside view of how these experiences have resulted in complicated grief, anxiety, anger, regret, and unforgiveness.

In their life review, they become aware that it is no longer okay to ignore it and may try to make amends with those on earth to free both souls from being stuck in unresolved emotional states. Even if you never asked for one, receiving an apology that is heartfelt, sincere, and directly for you can release you from holding onto negative emotions that prevent you from fully experiencing the goodness in your life. Receiving an apology is a profound experience, and it is possible because, in the afterlife, there is clarity and the desire to clear unsettled emotions between you and others, soul-to-soul.

In many circumstances, one apology can transform a life. It can provide comfort, reassurance, and acknowledgment of your feelings as valid, real, and true. Other times, multiple apologies over the years are sometimes given, especially if the hurt occurred over decades or a lifetime. As an apology settles within you, peace arrives, too, with the nature of your relationship to this person. Your heart begins its healing, and when the thought or mention of this person arises it no longer causes a visceral negative reaction but a more neutral or positive one.

Soulful Suggestion

Begin by writing a letter to someone in spirit who has knowingly or unknowingly hurt you and with whom you wish to receive communication that leads to healing. Write about your experience, the hurt, disappointment, rejection, or whatever you are still holding onto that still pains you. Ask your guardian angels and spirit guides to assist in protection and facilitate a healing exchange that is in your best interest currently. Allow yourself to feel as if healing is genuinely possible and desired by both parties. Sit undisturbed, close your eyes, and imagine what it would be like to receive an apology or forgiveness from this person.

How would your life change? How would your life be improved? How would it change the direction of your life? How would this healing make you feel?

In meditation, imagine yourself greeting this person and having a relatable conversation that is reassuring to you. Sit with them and let them express to you what's in their heart with words or sentiments that foster healing in the moment. As the conversation begins, listen, but also begin journaling the words, messages, or impressions you are receiving from this exchange.

Let it be one of transformational healing and closure of the unresolved pain you have carried for so long. When you are finished writing, thank this person and your personal spiritual team for assisting you in healing from emotions important to your well-being.

Having the kind support of family and friends on earth and in the spirit realm is crucial to your healing process. Forgiveness of yourself and your loved one can provide a feeling of peace in your body. Loving yourself while doing your best to keep your heart open to forgiveness allows you to feel loved and valued.

Gratitude

Each day in life is unique, just like you. May you see it with bright, sparkling eyes and feel it with your whole heart and being. Having the awareness that you are worthy to receive blessings and ease in real-time can involve all aspects of your life, from home, health, wealth, freedom, friendships, peace, and love. When you ask for something that is meaningful to you, ask in a way that feels right to you, but mostly ask for the feelings that these things bring to you and your life. Trust that you deserve them, will receive them, and be grateful for the opportunity to have them as if they are already received.

Gratitude can evoke a feeling of wonder and appreciation for the grace of receiving that which you may need, strive for, or request in your healing journey. Gratitude has a way of attracting more to be grateful for when you tune into its appearance and effects on your life. It is the law of attraction in action: more begets more, and it multiplies. Giving thanks is a universal practice for that which you receive in advance, at the time, or afterward. It all works the same. Offering a thank you to the universe, to God, to your spirit team, and to your loved ones in this life and the afterlife is a generous thing to do as you show appreciation for their love, guidance, protection, and support. Offering a heartfelt thank you to the people in your life who have impacted or cared for you in loving ways is a beautiful gesture that yields significant rewards.

My own grieving heart is repeatedly uplifted by the compassionate encouragement of my Soulful Starlight daughters, my spiritual guidance team, and time in prayer, along with a weekly session with my mediumship circle with the JOYS. Spending quality time with my husband, family, and friends is always mindfully appreciated.

Soulful Suggestion

Gratitude is a constant thing to keep in your mind. Throughout the day, be aware of everything that comes to you that you appreciate. And give thanks for it. Go to bed with gratitude in your heart and mind for the things that brought joy or comfort to your life.

Receiving Ashes

On a Friday in late July, I received word that Crystal's ashes were ready to be picked up. I totally lost it on the call. Thankfully, I was at a lovely friend's hair salon, just her and I, as my emotions melted down. Over the next few days, I struggled in reaching out to her uncle, who could assist in this matter. However, remarkably, in a sincere gesture of kindness, he phoned to inform me that he had already stopped by on his own to pick up her ashes and would stop by to deliver them when I was ready.

I was filled with a great sense of relief that I didn't have to drive two hours each way and then drive home in an emotionally distraught state of mind. Her uncle had graciously offered to drive to our home with her "riding shotgun" in the front of his pickup. He let me know that he stopped at a beach to let the dogs swim, and he placed her box on the tailgate out in the sun and ocean breeze alongside him. I was grateful for his kindness and sensitivity as I know he always tried to look out for her and showed great respect to me.

The night before he arrived at our home, my anxiety ramped up with each passing hour. As I was preparing for her arrival, I noticed it strangely felt like other times when I anticipated her visit, only this time, I was acutely aware of how different it would be.

I meditated and prayed for peace, acceptance, strength, and comfort before I drifted off to sleep late that night. In the early morning hours, I could hear her call out to me in my dream state, sounding exactly like she did when she had something important to say. There was a sense of urgency and intensity in her voice, coupled with a profound protectiveness that I could feel. Her concern for my well-being was real.

Throughout the next few hours, I could hear her reassuring me that she was okay and that she would be with me when I received her ashes and hold them in my arms. She let me know that she would have her arms around me while I cried and that she would provide strength to get through this emotionally surreal experience.

Repeatedly, she comforted me and assisted in calming my anxiety and anticipated fear of the emotional pain of having her returned to me in this state.

She emphatically sought to bolster my spirits by expressing that there was nothing that could have prevented her passing at that time.

When you think of me, please remember me as that vivacious, happy girl I could be. Don't think of me as the weak and troubled soul I could also be at times.

Her visit in my dreams was immensely helpful as I prepared for and awaited her arrival. "Just pick her up and talk to her, and it will be okay," her uncle said as I slightly shied away from the white shopping bag with her ashes he was holding out and offering to me.

I let him take a few steps toward the front door, and I gently took the bag from him and carried it up the stairs, through the front door, and into the house. I hugged the bag and set it down on a temporary place I had cleared on the corner of my desk in the living room of our small seaside cottage.

After her uncle hugged me goodbye and left, I let my husband know that I needed some private time with my daughter to just sit, hold her, and cry.

I felt my daughter's presence and began speaking to her as I grasped the handle on the white paper bag, lifted it up, and carried her into our bedroom.

I sat on the edge of the bed, clutched the small, heavy white box tightly to my chest, and instinctively began rocking back and forth like when she was a baby. Tears streamed down my face, and I sobbed as hard as I have ever had while allowing myself to feel strengthened and comforted by having her back home with me. After my lower back began to ache from the weight of the box, I stretched out on my bed with her box under my arms, and I cradled her as the tears flowed. I placed my first kiss on her box of ashes, wiped my tears, and sat up in bed.

Dear Mom, I feel your soul with me. We have been connected for many lives. Our hearts are bonded forever in time. The simplicity of life was not so for me. I chose a complicated life with you. I felt your pain, and you felt mine, yet I couldn't fix you, and you couldn't save me at the time we had together. We soothed each other, and it always felt comforting to be reunited with you from when I was a baby, being passed back and forth in our co-parenting arrangement. We had many lessons and learned early how to disconnect and reconnect again and again. As a child, I had to learn how to separate from you, to compartmentalize my feelings, and to live happily despite my difficult situations, and remarkably, so did you. I was always proud you were my mom, and I never wanted to disappoint you as I know you struggled with so much already. But I couldn't help it. It was a constant struggle to keep from spiraling down. You and "Bob" were my lifelines, and because I could always count on you, that kept me living longer than I probably would have otherwise. I wanted to be well, to make you proud, and to be an inspiration to others in recovery. At times, it seemed like it could be a reality, but the darkness always came knocking, and I needed to push it away. Giving to others through cooking was a passion we shared that I learned from you.

My dear daughter, I ask that you continue to be a part of my life. My life feels best when I can still feel your presence around me. I miss you so much, my sweet girl. Please know that you are immensely loved and that I am grateful to be your mom. I only wish we could have smiled more and stressed less through all the chapters we faced together.

Emotional Release

There are times in your grief journey when the most healing thing you can do for yourself is to lean into your grief.

By this, I mean to let yourself feel what your heart and soul are trying to say. Observe the feelings and emotions you experience as you let yourself ease into the hurt carried within you. Is it regret, resentment, anger, sadness, loneliness, or something else?

Try to identify the most intense feeling that comes to the surface. Let yourself open up to allow the painful emotions to breathe in fresh air, light, and love.

As I was standing in the kitchen preparing food one day, suddenly, I was overcome with intense emotions dating back to the birth of my daughter, Crystal. It was like being regressed to the time and place of her birth, infant years, and young childhood. I became engulfed in sorrow, guilt, and regret for not protecting her enough, no matter how hard I tried. It was a traumatic and sad childhood for a bright, joyful, and beautiful blue-eyed baby girl. I felt this regret deep in my soul, and I wished with all my heart that life would have been better for her. The childhood wounds she endured were carried in her body, heart, and soul throughout her life, which ended suddenly in her thirties.

The experience of reliving these painful times was necessary for my soul's growth to release long-held emotional pain for things I could not control. It was time to release the heavy burden that I carried and to allow a heart opening to take place, freeing my body to heal and regenerate, thus allowing more love to be experienced and felt in my life at this time. As the pain peaked, I leaned into it, offering myself compassion and love, and began visualizing it being released from my emotional body into pure healing energy. I asked my angels and guides to let light and love fill those empty places, uplifting my state of body and mind.

Over the years, I did much inner work in clearing, balancing, and releasing long-held emotions in my body, spirit, and soul. It was deep work, letting go of layers of grief, sadness, and loss, as well as anything else that no longer served my highest good or wasn't mine to carry. During the days of intense grief work, I felt very introspective as I implemented Reiki energy, exercise, prayer, mediumship, intuitive writing, and nurturing food and beverages, and I shed many tears. Afterward, I managed to emerge from the darkness, feeling reawakened with a renewed sense of hope and light streaming into my life again.

My desire to share this love, light, and hope with you also returned in soulful resilience. In my personal experience, I found it helpful to be conscious and aware of how I am relating to the experience of traumatic loss. As early as possible in your grief journey, I encourage you to begin writing your emotions as they come up in a journal and to begin releasing the pain and suffering.

I can relate if you feel overwhelmed, unable to focus your thoughts, or still feeling numb in your heartbreak. It is natural to feel scattered and to have your memories seem like they blur together. Just do your best to express whatever you can that's in your heart, so that you give your grief room to breathe.

Soulful Suggestion

Let these powerful emotions move through you. Keep breathing deeply.

Don't allow yourself to get stuck here. Let the hurt and sadness float away.

Visualize yourself being surrounded by a bubble of white light protecting you from fear and anxiety, allowing only peaceful, joyful, hopeful, and uplifting thoughts and feelings to permeate it. You may have tools or techniques that you found helpful through difficult times. Consider whether any of those can be beneficial to you today. Be mindful of your self-reflection and self-talk. Learn to love and accept yourself. Make peace with who you are and with all you have experienced.

Asking for Help

Grief is complicated, and your grief deserves to be heard. If at any time you are not feeling supported in your healing process, reaching out to others familiar with grief can be beneficial to you. Whether you choose individual counseling, grief therapy, or support groups online or in person, you will not feel so alone as you grieve. Some people find it helpful to talk to someone early after suffering a great loss, and others wait differing amounts of time to seek additional support. I would encourage you to look for a provider or group that will help you discover ways to heal as you learn to cope, allowing you to reflect on how you can gradually find moments of peace and self-compassion in creative ways.

Questions to ask yourself:
- Are you being honest with yourself about how you are feeling, experiencing, and processing your grief?
- Do you desire more time alone or with others, and in what way?
- Are you being gentle and empathetic to your grieving heart and soul?
- Are you able to accept love, support, and kindness from others, or do you push them away?
- Are you feeling loved and cared for by at least one loved one or friend?
- Are you able to be generous and helpful to others who need you?
- Are you using your skills, talents, and interests in a hobby or craft you enjoy?
- Is your general mood pleasant, intense, serious, moody, resilient, calm, or angry?
- Have you set an intention for restorative well-being in the wake of loss?
- Have you forgiven yourself and or your loved one since their passing?
- Do you allow yourself to feel uplifted by lighthearted entertainment?
- Do you give yourself respect for your courageous and conscious strength?
- Do you offer nurturing to another person or pet as well as yourself?
- Do you feel isolated or surrounded by your family, and how does it make you feel?

- Are you taking care of your physical health with nutritious food and activity?
- Are you finding comfort in or expanding your spiritual beliefs?
- Are you encouraging yourself to keep learning, growing, and improving?
- Can you find something to be grateful for each day?
- Do you allow yourself to experience healing in soulful, inspired adventures?
- Have you hugged yourself today?
- Are you allowing yourself to sit in the stillness of meditation?
- Have you expressed gratitude to the people who have impacted your life in meaningful ways?

Soulful Notes

Seventeen
Soulful Self-Love & Self-Care

"Set your daily intention for soulful self-care as you look for opportunities, gestures or experiences that uplift your current state of mind and emotions to one that is more comforting to you."

—**Nancy Yuskaitis**

Soulful Self-care is about listening to your body and heeding its need for rest, nutrition, and rebalancing to allow for greater healing. Giving yourself permission to practice Soulful Self-care is a gift that will keep providing uplifting sustenance to your life.

When you experience grief and loss, it sets you in a mode of self-survival. Your world becomes very narrow as you struggle to heal from this trauma. Self-preservation is necessary at this fragile time to build up your strength, courage, and resiliency. Soulful Self-care can ease your journey through this process, which has been quite turbulent for some time.

Along with providing nurturing care for yourself, it can be quite beneficial to be mindful of noticing something beautiful, enjoyable, or inspiring in your surroundings, even if it is only mildly so at first.

The uplifting and positive effects can be felt immediately and are also cumulative in their improvement of your well-being.

In the first year after loss and for several beyond, your physical and emotional energy may feel diminished, and activities you may have previously enjoyed will often change, at least temporarily, while you are deeply grieving. You may have little or no extra energy for your favorite activities, hobbies, or even your job. Some days, it took every bit of energy I could muster within me to rise and face another day without Crystal. It literally required living moment to moment with lots of self-care and self-love to keep going.

Many people find relief in yoga, running, swimming, biking, and working out at the gym, but certainly if these activities are too intense, I discovered just going on a leisurely walk can be helpful and beneficial on the days you feel up to it. Raising your energy and keeping it elevated improves your physical function and well-being to fight off the heavy weariness that often descends while you are grieving.

Along with sleep, I found that my body and spirit responded well to therapeutic massage and Reiki healing energy at the hands of a compassionate and skilled professional.

I can tell you from personal experience that the gift of self-care in the skilled hands of a chiropractor, massage therapist, esthetician, or lightworker is a profound experience for a grieving heart. Setting an intention for the session and giving someone the opportunity to assist you in your process of healing, balancing, and uplifting your body and spirit is highly beneficial for improving the way you feel on multiple levels. The decade I worked passionately as a licensed therapeutic massage therapist and Reiki practitioner was enlightening in just how powerful bodywork can be for those in emotional or physical pain.

After a session, the calming effect is very noticeable, but I would be remiss if I didn't also mention that as the therapist works deeply on your body, there may be an emotional response from you in the form of tears. At least there was for me in a few of the sessions and once for my massage therapist while she was working on me. I wasn't aware of it until she mentioned it afterward, but she could feel the grief I carried was so intense that even she began to cry while working on me.

If you feel emotional, don't hold your emotions back. Just let the tears come, soft and gentle or intensely raw. It will not feel especially pleasant at the time, but once you are through the emotional release, you will feel immensely calmer and lighter. Massage provides a nurturing experience that soothes your frayed emotions, offers you a positive, soulful, inspired adventure to look forward to, and also offers the encouragement you may need to feel more supported.

My Reiki practice, which began decades ago, has sustained my life through devastating changes and challenges of every kind by assisting in rebalancing my energy, providing healing to my heart, and strengthening my weary spirit. It also fuels my light-filled mission as a Reiki master, medium, and life coach to not only survive trauma but also to light the path for others on a similar journey.

One winter day in Crested Butte, Colorado, as I gazed out the window watching the snow fall ever so lightly, then speed up quickly and consistently, it reminded me of how loss can be in the beauty, resilience, and continued determination one must have to live with a grieving heart. Just when you think that you have acclimated to the pace of your life, it changes quickly, like the pattern of snowfall. Emotions change direction and intensity quickly, like falling snow, and one must learn to regain their balance through the shifting emotional changes of their experience. This allows grief and sadness to be released through acknowledgment, expression, bodywork, prayer, meditation, energy work, creativity, and journaling.

Self-love and soulful self-care can provide immense nurturing, healing, and comfort to you in these sorrowful times. Taking special care of yourself is crucial to your progress as you begin your grief journey and beyond.

In our complex lives, most people don't take the time to ask themselves important questions and listen for the answers.

Questions to ask yourself:

- How am I feeling right now?
- What could possibly help me to feel better in this sad situation that I cannot change?
- What could possibly add lightness or provide comfort in my grieving as I observe the heavy weight of sadness I am carrying?

Soulful Notes

As you wake each day, check in with yourself and ask your soul what is needed for improved comfort in your life today. Ask again at bedtime so that transformative healing can be done while you sleep.

When you wake, listen for the answer and promise yourself that you will take special care of yourself. Watch the sunrise or go for an early morning walk to refresh your senses. Read an uplifting passage, poem, or chapter from a book or blog that provides a promising start, middle, or end to your day. Journal about your experiences, how you feel, and what you would like to achieve in your process of transforming your grief into one that lives more comfortably with you, a softer, more peaceful grief. Allow space in your life for doing things you love. Develop a connection with your desires and goals. Create a relationship with yourself that is a treasured one.

By honoring your grief and giving it the attention it needs to heal, it will renew your energy, encouraging you to take the scenic route, try something new, and gain a fresh perspective.

Make time to ground yourself to the earth and let the brilliant beams of light move through you upward, and let the energy of the stars move down to your heart space, filling it with sparkling light and comforting your feelings of heartbreak and loss with a healing balm.

As you sit or walk in nature, let it be a healing experience. As you breathe in the lovely sights, scenes, and sounds around you, let the sun nurture your being and comfort the unhealed parts of you. Let the fresh air breathe new hope and possibility into your soul as you inhale the energy of goodness and exhale the heaviness of grief.

Love and Marriage

"Emotional availability—what a precious gift to those we love."

—Nancy Yuskaitis

Love transforms lives. Love is the greatest equalizer. It gives life to any situation. The energy of loving feels good and is transferable to uplift others, too. Love is the most important experience in life. Giving, receiving, and feeling loved open our hearts, soothe our wounds, and provide great joy, peace, and comfort to us.

Love teaches us to express kindness and compassion in loving gestures through our words, actions, and touch and fills us with amazement for life's adventures.

Love expands the experiences we share with others, and grief is one of those experiences. Grief also has the power to separate. In fact, many relationships do not survive the loss of a child as each parent grieves differently. One may feel the need to express and share their feelings and memories, and the other may shut down all communication relating to their grief.

When Lavender passed away, I was very young and wasn't prepared to deal with the pain of grief as I struggled in a challenging marriage, yet I persevered so I could begin every day as a loving, present, and capable mom to my young son and later my daughter. It took several additional major events, including my subsequent divorce, several relocations, remarriage, and the ten-year anniversary of my child loss, before I came to realize the extent of the unhealed grief held in my life. My intense sadness, trauma, and grief had caused the inability to feel happiness and joy. And that's when my healing became a major focus in my life.

After the initial loss of Crystal, I was comforted daily by my supportive husband, my daughter's longtime stepfather, who also deeply grieved her loss, yet my emotional availability was diminished in an act of self-preservation. Stepparents also provide a different perspective and experience to consider and may feel the loss in different ways depending on many factors.

Family Relationships

Based on the relationship with the loved one who has passed and the emotional ability to process, heal, and be supportive, is a question where the answer is different for each family. If you have the support, encouragement, and love of at least one family member, friend, or support system who believes in you, let that love fill the empty places within your heart to comfort and soothe you.

If this person is a loved one, then you must remember that patience, compassion, and understanding need to come from both sides, as it is difficult and draining to support a grieving person full-time.

I felt as if my happiness center was gone and that a part of me was missing, leaving my emotions flat and gray. Life seemed dull, empty, and so very quiet without Crystal. I didn't know if I would ever experience joy again. It seemed impossible to imagine my life without her warmth and zest for life.

As the days went by, I struggled with the quietness of my life without her buoyant personality, and I appreciated the calls and visits from my son and his wife and my brother and sister-in-law. Yet, it was the reminders from Crystal that she was still with me that were deeply consoling.

Friendship

The warmth of friendship is beyond compare. Whatever stage or age you may be in, it's important to be mindful of the social aspect of relationships. The quality of our friendships gives meaning to our life experiences. The value we place on experiences with friends adds depth and beauty to our world. Longtime friendships offer comfort in the familiarity of personalities and can provide reassurance that we are loved and lovable just the way we are. New friendships provide the opportunity to be ourselves as we are in the present as we grow together in shared common interests.

The benefit of having someone to walk a healing path with you is immense. It is not necessary for this person or persons to have experienced a similar occurrence. It only requires an open heart, a caring nature, a desire for your highest well-being, and a comforting presence to reassure you that you have the strength and the support to survive this heartbreak.

I have one such friend, "Cynthia," whose friendship spans over four and a half decades of life experiences that include a blended family, love, divorce, children, parenting, remarriage, child loss, illness, and family separation and yet is always filled with empathy, encouragement, kindness, compassion, respect, and understanding. This friendship that began in a most unusual manner created a bond that I've treasured and has helped each of us to survive many difficult and challenging circumstances with unconditional love. I will always be grateful for and cherish this relationship with my friend, her husband, her daughter, and her family.

As I was completing the first draft of this book, I received a message from a childhood friend with a request to give her a call. "Kim" had been a close friend during our teenage years growing up in Miami, Florida, and was even in my wedding when I married my childhood love at seventeen. We remained close into our twenties, and then, honestly, we lost contact as she and her husband continued their friendship with my ex-husband over many decades. In our teens, there was a group of us that were close, yet time moved on, and we each married or divorced and remarried, and my ex-husband kept closely in touch with these same friends. I would only remain close with one, and he and I, with our spouses, enjoyed great times in the Florida Keys, Crystal Beach, and Crested Butte, Colorado.

When my ex passed away in 2015, fate would bring Kim and me back together at his celebration of life in the Florida Keys. It was a reunion in which we enjoyed reconnecting, even on this sad occasion. When she contacted me this time, it was to share about the passing of one of our mutual friends. Throughout the following days, Kim and I recounted stories, exchanged photos, and reminisced about those days of our youth in South Florida. As we conversed, I knew she was grieving and that she would appreciate receiving a message from our friend who recently joined the afterlife.

I asked my angels, spirit guides, and Soulful Starlights to assist in providing a message that would be reassuring to her and his heartbroken friends. Soon, a message came through, and I sat down to transcribe it. At first, I was given the confirmation that it was my ex who brought our newly departed friend to talk with me as he became aware of my mediumship after his passing from our daughters, the Soulful Starlights.

During multiple sessions of afterlife communication, he and I had made great strides in healing our dysfunctional relationship in life through automatic writing, and at this time, I was grateful to him for bringing forward our newly departed friend in the afterlife.

I listened to this mutual friend describe his new realization that we are all given the opportunity to remain close to our loved ones, to watch over them, and to offer guidance and protection, but first, he needed to become acclimated in his new environment, in his words, of unlimited beauty.

I was very excited to receive and share these comforting messages for Kim and our other friend with welcoming responses. As soon as I completed the calls, I went downstairs to see my husband by the pool, and immediately, we observed something we'd never noticed before in two sweet bunnies sitting in our fenced-in backyard with us. A mystical, magical, and mindful moment of confirmation that my Soulful Starlights were sending their continued presence in our lives.

Bunny sightings have been a common occurrence since very early in Crystal's passing, and they have been known to show up in places where you wouldn't expect to see one, and some even stay for hours. At times, one will be standing at the corner of our street when we drive home or waiting in our front or backyard. Other times, one will come close on a walk and gently stay. It's always uplifting and delightful and truly feels heaven-sent by Crystal.

A Kind Afterlife Message

Dave is a tender-hearted soul who was still alive when Crystal passed away. To acknowledge and shine a light on her transition to spirit, I asked our family and friends on social media to please light a candle for her on a certain day and to send photos to me to feel closer to those around the world. Dave went above and beyond by hiking to a mountaintop with candles, flowers, and a beautiful poem he shared with me. I was so grateful. After his passing, we communicated several times, and this is one of his messages to me as I thought about him on his birthday.

Thanks, Nanc, thanks for the birthday wishes. Life is good. Here, I'm on my way to doing some really good things. Helping people, ya know, to acclimate when they pass due to alcohol addiction. I see your daughter, Crystal, she works in this area, too. We chuckle about you sometimes and shine a light on some silly signs we send you. The yellow Jeeps with the ducks are one of our favorites.

About Crystal, she is amazing. What a caring, exuberant soul she is. I can feel you in her heart. She's so proud of you. Your life has had some physical struggles of late. Know they will be resolved in due time without much effort. Release from your body and cells any trauma still residing there that has a hold on you. Trauma from those years in your thirties of immense stress, pull them from the grip your body has on them and fill those holes with love and light and healing energy.

You must repel these stressors to allow your body to thrive again. Be at peace in all you do. Your work to inspire others will continue despite your lower energy now. Keep expressing and working toward the completion of your book. I can see it finished in glowing book form. Soon, you will, too! Know that you have a message that will touch hearts. Keep digging deep and finding ways to describe it. Your team is assembled to assist and ready to go. You are not alone in this journey. Much love & light, always.

Kindness

"I choose to heal by allowing my soul to get in the flow as I expand, transform, and blossom."

—Nancy Yuskaitis

The kind support of family and friends is crucial to your healing process. The amazing thing is that even a simple gesture can have lasting effects. I genuinely appreciated the caring attention I received in my early loss from my sister-in-law in frequent, thoughtful text messages offering love and encouragement straight from her heart.

There have been other times in recent years when a gesture of kindness felt immensely comforting to my grieving heart. One of these times was when my husband and I were driving back home after being out West. As we were southbound on US1 in the Florida Keys, my anxiety was high, and my emotions had risen to the surface and bubbled over. Tears streamed down my face like a faucet I couldn't turn off. My husband looked at me with sympathy but also a little bit of exasperation. He had been looking forward to arriving back at our home, but I was dreading it. "I can't stop crying. I'm just emotional," I said.

My daughters in a box, I shouted through my tears. Knowing her box of ashes would be there to greet us when we walked in the front door, rather than her warm and bubbly personality, just hurt terribly. Immediately, I called out to my angels to lighten the energy between my husband and me in the car. The tension was laden with sadness and regret on both sides. Please sprinkle lightness over us as we travel to our Florida Keys home, I prayed. Soon, my cell phone rang. It was my son checking on us. Before he ended the call, he simply asked if I was excited about going home to the Keys. My response was immediate: "Going back home is an emotional experience that terrifies me."

"I know, he said."

At that moment, I felt comforted and understood by those kind words.

Compassion

Compassion creates an amazing and sometimes unexpected bonding experience between individuals who may be related in some way, acquaintances, or even complete strangers. While traveling home to Florida from Colorado for Crystal's celebration of life, one morning, I walked into a hotel restaurant where my husband was already seated at a table.

As soon as the server noticed I had arrived, she walked over and said, "Good morning, beautiful." I was startled by her friendliness as I certainly had never had anyone say that to me before in a restaurant. As we began chatting, my husband glanced at me with compassion and let her know that I had just lost my grown daughter. Without a moment's hesitation, she walked over and gave me a hug. Immediately, she began to share funny stories with us about her grown daughter.

As I looked into her eyes, she surprised me again by saying, I miss her. She passed away five years ago. Now, with tears in my eyes, I stood to give her a hug as I could see the deep pain she carried within her. At that moment, I could feel the immense compassion exchanged between us as we embraced, this time in mutual grief. When she walked away, she left me with a caring statement: "Us mothers must stick together."

I nodded in agreement and left breakfast that day, so awestruck by the poignant way in which we both were supported by our daughters in the spirit world, who just had to be smiling. It truly was an honor to meet this lovely soul.

I encourage you to consider in what ways compassion has touched your life and encouraged your healing process in living with loss in a gentler way.

Hearts and Rosebuds

"You have to bring my mom flowers for Valentine's Day," she said.

"Please, a little bouquet of pink roses because I loved pink and hearts, and I send her and my sister all my love."

As I walked home from a neighbor's house, I could hear in my mind her daughter in spirit making a special request for me to acknowledge her mother on the upcoming holiday. It was a few days before the big day, but I answered her request, understanding completely how the thoughtful gestures of flowers had helped me to heal as if they were heaven-sent gifts straight from my daughters. On the fourteenth, as I shopped for pink roses, I felt the caring presence of this lovely daughter assisting me in choosing the perfect bouquet to surprise her mom with hearts of love. Flower shopping is one of my favorite things to do with my Soulful Starlights, and they have assisted in choosing the perfect flowers to bring home many, many times. As I arrived at my neighbor's house to deliver the flowers, I greeted her with a bouquet of pale pink rosebuds with a hint of lavender and ruffled edges.

Upon seeing them, she immediately began to cry. I quickly expressed to her that these were from her daughter in heaven. As it turned out, not only was this day Valentine's Day, but it was also an anniversary for them. In addition, the flowers I was encouraged to bring to her were so perfect, as rosebuds were very sentimental to this mom. She had decorated the bedroom and dressed both of her little twin daughters in pink rosebud patterned dresses when they were babies, and this little one was also laid to rest in an outfit of beautiful rosebuds. It was heartwarming to share in this loving gesture between a daughter and her mother, blending our two worlds.

Creative Expression

You are a treasure to the universe. You are unique, and there is no one exactly like you. Your thoughts, experiences, talents, personality, grief, and heart are individually yours to express in ways that matter to you.

In my experience, holding protectively onto painful emotions is not the most comfortable way to heal and grow through grief and loss. I encourage you to be expressive in ways that soothe your soul, offer healing to your heart, and provide uplifting comfort to your body, mind, and spirit.

Creativity is an avenue to greater well-being. It is also soulful self-care.

Holding onto heavy emotions is restrictive and limits our ability to listen to our intuition, so I ask you to tune into your emotions and choose one or more to observe. Ask your soul how you can best express what's in your heart to achieve healing in your life. You may be encouraged to use color, words, signs, messages, symbols, etc., to express your emotions in imaginative ways. Give your full expression in a journal to capture its essence in whatever form you choose.

Questions to ask yourself:
- What does my soul need to express right now?
- What emotions am I holding onto that would better serve me to be released?
- What sensations am I experiencing in my body at this moment: tightness in my chest, fear of the present or future, uneasiness or discontent, anger, hurt, disappointment in my life, in others, or in world events?
- In what ways am I expressing my heartfelt emotions to family, friends, and the world in my healing journey? Is it through writing, talking, or interacting with others or through creative endeavors such as music, art, or movement?
- What activities, experiences, or adventures will help me move through and break free from the restraints of grief toward a feeling of emotional freedom?

Soulful Notes

Soulful Guideposts for Living with Loss

Let all emotions be acknowledged, move through me, and outward.
Listen to my heart, soul, and wise inner guidance.
Meditate daily or often.
Share quality time with loved ones in nurturing ways.
Get back to my center easily.
Hold myself accountable.
Realize in some situations that I've done all I can.
Surrender, turn it over to a higher power.
Accept rather than resist.
Allow good days and tough days, too.
Remain open to guidance from the spirit world.
Be kind and loving to myself.
Find reasons to live every day.
Start a gratitude-inspired adventure journal.
Enjoy life in small and large ways.
Keep expanding my consciousness.
Be a light and illuminate the way.
Trust that I am on the right path.

Eighteen
Special Days of Significance

→))))→

"The love that bonds us is stronger than the grief that separates us."

—**Nancy Yuskaitis**

At certain times, life gives you a variety of emotions to take in and experience. Events such as anniversaries, weddings, graduations, and vacations after loss offer poignant times to reflect and feel your loved one's presence. There may be sentimental memories that bring a smile to your heart, yet the grief is so intense that it can bring uncontrollable tears as you miss your loved one's presence deeply.

Anniversary Dates

As her anniversary approaches each year, I contemplate new ways to remember Crystal in hopeful, uplifting, and forward-moving ways that honor her life yet play a role in comforting my heart in the process.

On this past anniversary, I had been aware of Crystal's presence on a near-daily basis. Yet still, to be closer to her, I picked up the turquoise box in my office containing her ashes from the bookcase and squeezed it to my chest. In doing so, it was like receiving a hug in real life, in this life, right then when I needed it. This hug came with such a familiar feeling, it allowed me to experience the full essence of her vibrant personality. I could tell that she was infusing my spirit with her strength, resilience, hope, love, understanding, compassion, unbridled joy, creativity in the kitchen, soulful exuberance, and tenacity.

I also felt despair, then a throwing off and discarding of it. Next, I felt a resurgence of her being in spirit. I saw the light swirling around her and two angels, one on each side. They were my angels, and all three guided my path in re-emerging as a soulful practitioner and author who guides others by sharing lessons of living as I do so closely with the other side.

There is sadness and then light, and there is life again. My heart is open, and there is love radiating outward from the core of my being. My daughters are gone from this earthly life, and they are still with me from their place in the afterlife.

Hi Mom, I've been waiting to talk with you again. I completely understand how difficult these anniversary dates are for you. I am glad you are feeling strong today. I know what a powerful day it is and how hard you have worked to stay centered and brave. Your courage and tenacity do not go unnoticed.

Mother's Day

Receiving a personal message from a loved one in spirit is a special experience in every way. Receiving it at a significant time is especially healing, as in the situation with Denise.

Her mom's spirit message arrived in a Soulful Starlight Letter just before Mother's Day, which was the anniversary of her passing, unbeknownst to me, and it was filled with words of comfort and encouragement during an emotionally difficult time in her life. When the next Soulful Starlight Letter arrived, Denise was in the middle of repairs to her home after a tree had fallen on the roof. Her mom let her know that she not only knew about the incident but also protected her from being harmed that evening. Denise is grateful for the confirmation and peace she received in knowing we don't travel this world alone.

Mother's Day Flower

The year after we moved away from the Florida Keys, my husband and I traveled back to Key West for his birthday. We were enjoying our walk down Duval Street in and out of the quaint little gift shops we knew so well when suddenly, a little white flower fell from the sky a few inches in front of me. Instinctively, I lifted my hand up and caught the beautiful flower in my palm.

Quickly, I looked around and observed that there were no flowering trees nearby or any wind to explain its appearance, and without hesitation, I accepted it as a gift from my two daughters. I had already been receiving signs to let me know Crystal was with us on that trip, but receiving this flower gift was quite an extraordinary surprise. It was Mother's Day, after all, and what made it even more special was that even though I had always loved seeing the pink or yellow plumeria blossoms around the Keys, I had never observed a white one before that moment. The symbols of frangipani are strength to withstand tough challenges, intense love, and a connection with the spirit world. It was a sign that took my breath away as it filled my heart with love and gratitude at the same time. I continue to hold the essence of this flower close in my heart and memory, along with my two daughters in heaven.

Birthdays after Loss

Your own birthdays are not the same when your parents are gone and additionally, a spouse, child, or sibling. Yet certainly, life is worth celebrating, and so is creating a present and future filled with hope, reclaimed joy, and soulful resilience. A new relationship can take place with your loved one if you allow yourself to experience it.

On my first birthday without Crystal, I awoke and immediately began to meditate. Quickly, I realized there was a birthday party going on in heaven where all my deceased family were there, along with my spiritual guidance team. The large group assembled in front of me. Some were carrying festive signs, and others had balloons or gifts in their hands. Each had a message for me as they passed a microphone around from one to the other. It was a loving and powerful experience, I know Crystal orchestrated to lighten my grief on my special day.

Feather Cloud

Later, I ended the day looking out at the mountain view in our backyard. In vivid sunset colors, there was a gigantic feather-shaped orange cloud in striking contrast to the bluest of skies. It felt to be a lovely sign from my daughter beaming across the horizon.

As my second birthday approached without my daughter, my anxiety rose more each day without my sentimental child to acknowledge it. As my husband and I entered a restaurant in Santa Fe that night, sitting on a bench in the entryway was a big, bold, and beautiful peacock just waiting to surprise me. I was immensely grateful for the special sign that uplifted and delighted our celebration.

Despite my emotional overwhelm in anticipation of birthdays, when the day arrives, I discover that I am uplifted by the generosity, kindness, and love of my husband, family, and friends as I step into a new year with renewed hope, purpose, and passion for life in my journey with grief.

On another occasion, it was almost my birthday, a milestone one. A few weeks beforehand, I began to acclimate myself to this upcoming new age. I gave myself space to stretch into it and become familiar with how it would feel to be that age. I wanted to ease into a new chapter in a new decade of a new year.

I allowed my mind to review the various past decades of my life. I didn't go back as far as childhood, but I did begin in my teenage years to review key or pivotal points. My intention was to look at how far I had come along with the acceptance of the present life I live.

What happened, though, was that I stirred up old unresolved emotions and brought them to the surface again. In trying to live my life in a heart-centered and conscious way, the intensity of emotion caught me off guard like a wave of grief that knocks you over when you aren't expecting it. Over the course of this experience, I set out to consider what I had learned in my life up to this point. That also proved to be overwhelming and painful.

It felt like the heavy, weighted blanket of grief that I felt after Crystal's passing had been dropped on me again, and I was struggling to lift it before I succumbed to despair. I was overcome with anxiety and grief about the loss I had experienced of my two daughters, and I was worried about the well-being of my remaining child, my son, and our family.

Fear, panic, grief, regret, and sadness were all rushing through my emotional body, filling up all the space that would usually contain hope, joy, and gratitude for the blessings in my life. At this point, I implemented Reiki, prayer, mediumship, angel work, journaling, a walk in nature, and I shed many tears.

Inner grief work can be a process of clearing, balancing, and releasing long-held emotions in our body, mind, and spirit. It is a process of letting go of layers of grief, sadness, and loss and anything that no longer serves our highest good. The release of heartbreak and sorrow occurred in heavy sobs until there were no more left to release at this time. Before retiring upstairs to get some sleep, I sat down alongside the bookcase in my office where Crystal's Tiffany blue box of ashes sits, and I hugged it to my chest as an emotional attempt to feel closer to her on the night of my birthday, leaving it with a kiss.

I had been asking spirit to release emotions and experiences that no longer served me, but wow! When you experience the trauma of losing two children and other traumatic events, it is no easy task. My husband tried his best to let me go through this transformational work privately while trying to bring love and joy to my heavy spirit.

I found that the birthday love that surrounded me from family and friends around the globe uplifted and brightened my special day, even while in a deep process.

Through the night, my angels, spirit guides, and loved ones in the afterlife assisted in lifting the heavy weight of sorrow, ushering in the return of lightness and hope by morning.

My energy returned to a high level. My sparkle and radiance returned in my eyes and face. My heart opened to give and receive kindness, patience, and love. My passion returned for life. My desire to share love, empathy, and hope with others had also returned in Soulful Resilience.

> *Mom,*
>
> *Lavender and I want to wish you a beautiful birthday from heaven. We have watched you in all the stages and emotions you have experienced this birthday. We have sent you love, surrounded you in love, and offered comfort in your tearful times. Please realize that we are nearby, experiencing life through you, and we only send the best protective and loving light to you and our family. Let go of your fears and your reactions from recent and past trauma. Let yourself live free of restraints, fear, sadness, and regret. This life is beautiful. Look at this gorgeous day. You have so much to be grateful for. Let yourself enjoy life to the fullest. You will avoid some pain if you can accept all that is and not long for what is not. Be the best version of love, light, joy, and beauty that you can be. Toss the heaviness off that has returned recently. Throw it off vigorously. After you have cried many tears, bring back the lighthearted joy. Please, you will feel so much better when you do.*

I believe birthdays are meant to be celebrated, and with that sentiment, I must mention a very special birthday tradition that takes place every year within my JOYS mediumship group. When one of our birthdays arrives, we gather around on Zoom for a special celebration like no other. We sing, blow out candles, eat cake, and share with the birthday person what we love about them. It is our time to enthusiastically gush about this person and to share what we most admire about them. It is festive and loving and fills hearts with gratitude on all sides. We then share messages and impressions from the spirit world specifically meant for them. My Soulful Starlights are never far, and it's always a lovely, loving experience that uplifts and awakens hearts.

Holidays and Christmas

Whatever your religious background, the Holidays are a festive time of year. For a grieving parent or other loved one, the expression of holiday spirit does not exist in the same way as before experiencing this loss. There is sadness and grief that overwhelm the emotions and a regret that life will never be the same again.

Thoughts are narrowly focused on our loss and the way our child or loved one will not be here for this holiday or any other upcoming ones in the future. This brings a heartache so deep and painful that just surviving this loss is a monumental task at hand.

Cards filled with holiday joy don't get sent as there is no desire or energy to do so. Holiday trees may be decorated in memory of your loved one with ornaments that carry a sweet sadness and tears or are not done at all. Gatherings may occur as families try to carry on for the sake of young ones or other family ties, but thoughts are distracted, hearts are still grieving, and life has lost its luster.

On the first Christmas without Crystal, we were asked to babysit our two grandsons in their home for the week and then to host our annual family party. It was a festive time that I appreciated immensely and proved to myself again that grief and joy can both exist in our world at the same time.

Returning home, though, brought inconsolable pain as I curled up in bed, sobbing my heart out. The crush of reality hit so hard that I didn't know if I could survive it. It was Christmas Day, and I just wanted to see my daughter, Crystal, in our home. She was there, but instead of seeing her, I felt her presence with me, knowing that if I did not believe in life after life, I don't know how I would have survived that first year.

On the following Christmas, as I was decorating the tree, I uncovered two beautiful ceramic snowflake ornaments that were a gift from Crystal a few years prior. I gently lifted each one and kissed it as my daughter, in spirit, watched. I read the words across the front of each one stating, Love and Believe. Through my tears, I said, "Yes. I do believe and will love you, always."

I kindly invite you to take a special moment to remember a bereaved parent or other grieving souls in your life with extra love, hugs, a heartfelt card, and a memory of their loved one, especially during the holiday season.

New Year

Each day is a new day to begin anew. A new year offers the opportunity for fresh new experiences to uplift, heal, and reclaim joy in your life, and yet, a new year holds great weight attached to it.

When you are grieving a loss, the new year can have a sense of dread attached to it. For many, the advance of time on the calendar is not welcome. It signifies that another year has come and gone without your loved one here to share in its experiences. It places more distance between you and your loved one who has passed.

I understand that totally, and I was given another way to reflect on this that I find helpful. Let me explain. Although your loved one is gone from your sight, they are still alive in the afterlife, sending love, comfort, and support to you as you struggle to go on living, one day at a time. With this knowledge, I try my best to acknowledge having survived the previous year with courage and the effort that was necessary to live alongside grief. I mindfully embrace the beauty, adventure, love, and kindness in my world, which helps to carry me forward with my grief inside.

One idea I found helpful is to set your intentions for the new year, month by month. You can choose a particular word for each month beginning in January and a statement or two of your goals, or you can ask spirit to guide you in setting intentions for each month.

Wishing you inspiration in creating your own intentions for a new or remainder of the year.

Soulful Suggestion

You can start anytime; it's not required to wait for a new year. Here is a sample:

January: Preparedness—Be flexible and allow your strength to be felt by those who need it.

February: Renewal—Renew vows to be bolder, braver, and kinder to myself in new ways.

March: Transcend—Stay focused on love, light, and lessons in expansive and colorful adventures.

April: Playful—Let the sun shine inward and outward as I enjoy the beauty of Spring.

May: Honor—Take the time to acknowledge the people who add safety, beauty, and love to my life.

June: Excitement—Expand my outreach and desire for fun, adventure, and travel.

July: Nurture—Allow your being to immerse yourself in nature and to be outdoors often.

Overdose Awareness Day

You may not be aware of this somber day designed to remember those who have passed due to addictions and or an overdose and to offer support to their families.

One year, as I acknowledged the significance of the day, I received this message from my spirit team.

We send an abundance of comfort to calm you. Just the mention of it raises your blood pressure. It is a dreadful situation around the world, yet we send you hope that you realize your daughter's struggle is over.

She is reborn with a vitality and a strength she was unable to master in this life. She sends her eternal love and gratitude to you for all your intentions, assistance, and loyalty to her health, well-being, and beautiful soul.

She went through so much and thought of you always in times of rejoicing and renewal. In struggle and despair, she tried to protect you. She knew that, ultimately, you would feel you failed to save her, but it wasn't about you at that point to do so.

She had come to the end of her journey with addiction and had found peace. Now, she wants you to find the peace and healing necessary as you live out a much longer life experience. Take what you can of her deep into your soul. Her generous essence, her lighthearted exuberance, and the way she used her personality to assist others. Just like we may embody the essence of our parents, so it is with our children. We hold their essence with us to help us move forward in our lives.

Honoring Your Loved One

There are many ways to pay tribute to your loved one or to celebrate in memory of their life. Throughout the year, on birthdays and anniversaries, I consider ways to acknowledge and honor my daughters with some special actions or activities. Some being more temporary, and others are more permanent acknowledgments that may be done solo, with family or friends, and or to benefit others. On more than one occasion, I donated money to a shelter for women and children in Key West in memory of Crystal, who had a long and wonderful relationship with the founder and her family.

On a more recent acknowledgment of Crystal's birthday, I shared it with a special little girl.

Thank you for the birthday tribute and little ceremony with your granddaughter. She is such a light in your life. You thought I arrived at birth with a zest for life. Well, she has tenfold that enthusiasm. Kids know when they are loved, and she certainly feels that from you two and her family. Your hearts are connected and woven together.

There are unlimited ways to acknowledge the life of your loved one that fit their personality and your grief journey. I've included some suggestions for you to reflect on to create your own memories that are meaningful to you and celebrate the personality of your loved one. Of course, you may have already found a way that feels right to you. I'd love to hear about it.

Soulful Suggestions in Memory

- Purchase or create expressive art.
- Participate in activities they enjoyed.
- Plan a celebration of life in your own way.
- Wear jewelry as a tribute.
- Plant a garden or a tree.
- Arrange for or design yard art, a mandala, or a bench.
- Give gifts or donations of time or resources.
- Enjoy meals or baked goods that you enjoyed together.
- Create a Kindness Rock Garden.
- Decorate with flowers at home, garden, or grave.
- Toss rose petals in the ocean.

- Attend a concert or music event.
- Take a vacation or trip.
- Spread ashes in a meaningful location.
- Get a tattoo.
- Take a class, obtain a certification, or join a workshop.
- Donate a skill you possess.
- Give generously to a meaningful cause.
- Write poetry, a song, or book in tribute.
- Light a candle and ask others to join you in doing so.
- Create a grief altar.
- Attend a favorite sporting event.
- Pay it forward, generously.
- Create a photo album of memories.

Nineteen

Peace, Passion, Mindfulness, & Joy

"Mindfulness allows you to be present in the actual moment as you are living it. It brings your awareness to observe how you may be feeling physically and emotionally."

—***Nancy Yuskaitis***

One of my main missions is fostering mindfulness, as the benefits are immense.

Mindfulness is living consciously with the intent to tune into your body, mind, and soul while looking upon the present moment with openness and an immense possibility of wonder.

Mindfulness provides a way for you to pause and observe the natural environment around you, your home, relationships, cuisine, and activities, and it gives depth and appreciation to your life. The sky may be ablaze with color. The sun may be rising in anticipation of a new day, a songbird may greet you in the morning, and a flower may be blooming in the front yard that you've not noticed before the moment you see it. You may encounter a beautiful animal sighting or receive a sign from your loved one, such as a red cardinal or a blue jay, a cottontail bunny, or a monarch butterfly that catches your eye and causes you to pause in gratitude and amazement. As you walk outside your door, be mindful of the sights and occurrences that may uplift and delight your soul.

Mindfulness can be as simple as observing your indoor surroundings and noticing the details in your environment. Look around at the colors of the walls and floors and let your eyes drift around the room until they settle on an item that brings about a positive feeling or memory in your emotions and mind. Allow the feeling it invokes to increase in the form of a story about how you came by this decorative item or artwork. If it was a gift, think about the person who gifted it to you and the positive feelings that were exchanged along with the gift. If it was something you yourself purchased, reflect on the pleasant experience of discovering this item and the excitement you felt bringing it into your home. Let these positive feelings double in size, then triple in size until the good vibes are bursting in your heart and your lips turn up in a smile. You can read much more about how mindfulness can have a positive effect on your journey in the chapter on Soulful Inspired Adventures.

Soulful Suggestions

- Be fully present right now.
- Develop more self-compassion.
- Experience increased peacefulness and calm.
- Realize that thoughts come and go.
- Become less reactive to unpleasant situations.
- Accept the possibility of comfort in the experience.
- Discover the beauty in the bittersweet.
- Experience beautiful moments of uplifting joy.
- Live life with more intention and focus.
- Discover enjoyment in everyday situations.

Finding Peace

> *"May we remember our loved ones in peace and allow the love and comfort we receive from them to uplift our grieving hearts."*
>
> *—Nancy Yuskaitis*

Developing a friendship with yourself is critical to your healing process as you go through your grief journey. Observe the weight of grief you are carrying in your heart and body. Is it heavy, or is it feeling a bit lighter today? Ask yourself what steps you can take to release this blanket of sadness and heartache. Allow the answers to come with love and compassion for yourself.

In your journal, list as many things as you can that may offer a little relief for your grieving heart. Is it a walk in nature, a tea date with a friend, planting new flowers in your garden, reading an inspiring book, listening to your favorite musician, cozying up on the couch with your loyal pet, or another uplifting experience or adventure?

Soulful Notes

As you do any one of these activities, let it be a healing experience. Let it nurture your being and comfort the unhealed parts of you. You may want to journal about how you feel and ask your spirit team to guide you in the steps to take to live more comfortably with your grief as you learn to love and accept yourself and make peace with all that you have experienced.

Reclaiming Joy

Joy is a feeling that one must nurture by engaging in harmonious pursuits.

On the days when feelings of joy are not possible, it's imperative to look for anything that will upgrade your emotions to a more comfortable state of being. Immerse yourself in that experience, even briefly. Let yourself go. Breathe. Observe. Receive.

Grief can be so overwhelming; its hold on you is so strong that it keeps you in the dark unless you go where the light is. When my Soulful Starlights prompted me out into the light, I sought the brightest and most vivid sun-drenched shades of color to immerse my being in and used them as an escape. As a form of color therapy, I allowed the colors to change the energy around me, and I felt uplifted by the joy these happy colors provided.

Reclaiming joy is not about putting on a happy face for others. It is something you do for yourself. It is where you consciously choose to find a reason to smile in your everyday reality. Doing so improves your well-being and opens you up to receiving lightness and moments of joy, even while missing your loved one immensely. The next time you smile, do so with the awareness that you can and will live with the emptiness you feel inside your heart. It is possible, I discovered, and I hope you will discover your own way to do so. One of the ways that worked best for me is to feel secure that my loved ones are happy and safe in the afterworld. They are just out of sight, yet close in heart, and they wish for us to be safe, happy, and well.

I ask you to choose to feel joy for yourself. You deserve to live joyously in peace and comfort. Give yourself permission to live, laugh, and love again with mindful intention in memory of your loved one.

Start by allowing yourself to look away from the pain for a few moments of relief as you observe something you find beautiful. It may be a setting in nature or a compassionate gesture. It may even be something you read, do, or watch, such as a movie, comedy, or concert. Each day, let yourself be swept away for a time in something that uplifts and inspires you.

Allow a soulful, inspired adventure in art, music, reading, learning, a sign from spirit, or basking in nature's beauty to bring a smile to your heart with an increased feeling of enjoyment. Let it ripple through your life.

During times when I am feeling overwhelmed by grief and upsetting situations beyond my control, I take a moment to sit or lie down and be still. I encourage myself to just breathe. In and out calmly. I set the intention of breathing in hope and goodwill into my spirit and to breathe out pain and sadness.

I honor my feelings, and I also allow myself to be nurtured with the positive energy found in close friendships, compassion, and empathy of those who have walked a similar path. I ask for the caring presence of angels, guides, and loved ones in spirit to assist in my healing journey.

Giving your heart the opportunity to experience reclaimed joy and hopefulness in the wake of loss takes conscious and mindful intention. Your life and well-being are worth every bit of attention you give them as you process your grief.

Soulful Grief Reflections

I'm sure you would agree that grief is heavy, and it can feel like a huge weight is sitting on your chest, preventing you from even getting out of bed, knowing your loved one is no longer living. The darkness can loom close, draining your energy physically and emotionally. Some days, it took everything I could muster to rise and face another day without my daughter. This left me living moment to moment and requiring an abundance of self-care and self-love to keep going, and that is when I was shown by my Soulful Starlights a way to increase my well-being and participate in discovering the little joys that made my broken heart feel uplifted.

In practicing a form of mindfulness while in the throes of grief, I trusted that if this was beneficial to me in lightening my heavy grief of child loss, then sharing it with others would be my next path. Giving back while in the process of healing accelerates your progress while providing a renewed sense of purpose and passion.

Passion is something that comes from inside a person. It is fueled by a desire to create, build, or manifest something important to you. It can be a dream, a new idea, or an intention to fulfill a calling you may have to help others.

Life has a way of reminding us where to put our attention and focus for the next phase of our lives. Let yourself imagine what it would be like to see yourself following this passion. Let your mind wander and see if you can get in touch with the emotions involved in starting this new venture. Try to get in touch with how you feel while picturing yourself engaged in this pursuit of yours.

Soulful journaling is a way to tap into your intuition and creativity in discovering renewed purpose and passion and can provide the impetus to share it with others.

Remember, your dreams are important to your soul's growth. Daydreams are filled with the desires of the spirit. Your spirit may be crying out for you to explore something new; can you do it? Listen to your heart, and you will find the answer.

Feeling called to give back while in the throes of grief as part of a process to heal, to grow, and to inspire others on a similar path is important to me. As I was experiencing deep grief, I trusted that my discovery of ways to uplift and lighten my grief would be beneficial to others. Giving back after feeling successful at something is a common experience, yet assisting others while in the process of grieving is a different type of motivation that some of us pursue.

In previous times in my life, I believed that our attitude was at the top of the list for achieving our goals. I've learned, however, that intention plays a bigger role than we might realize. To discover your renewed purpose or passion, consider what brings you enthusiasm that is so big it overflows outward from your heart out into the world. If you allow yourself to expand and shine rather than retreat and retract, you will find that you feel empowered to proceed. Ask for assistance from your angels and guides, and be patient as the process unfolds.

Years after I immersed myself in becoming a Reiki practitioner and massage therapist, I felt called to pursue certifications as a Reiki master and also in advanced mediumship, therapeutic art, spiritual life, and happiness coaching, all to foster ongoing healing in my own life and to one day encourage others to live uplifted and resilient lives beyond loss and through challenging life circumstances.

My intention for each day is to live my purpose in peace and passion for my two daughters as I feel their loving presence alongside me. Allowing yourself to rediscover a sense of purpose and passion may be the next step for you in your grief journey.

You have changed, and that which you used to enjoy at work, home, or in your free time may also change in subtle or significant ways. The passion I felt as a glass artist and jewelry designer sharing a love of design in Reiki-infused necklaces, earrings, and bracelets was derailed after Crystal's passing. She was my biggest fan, and without her, my inspiration pivoted as I then felt inspired to share my creativity with others through photography, graphic art, and inspirational writing. I found this new direction gave me something to look forward to and offered the focus I desired in helping others. In service, we discover our generosity of spirit and our ability to share love, light, and compassion as we grow.

Now That You Are Gone

I don't know who I am without you.
My purpose in life has been to guide you
through all the chapters in your life.
To rejoice in your joys and to comfort and,
encourage in your disappointments.
Now that you are gone, I must find my way,
through my tears and learn to live differently.

Soulful Starlight Grief Message

I see you try your best to accept others to be welcoming, and at times, it is uplifting for you, and other times it is draining. Your heart has been broken so many times and is giving you great physical pain that must be released over and over. It's not a one-and-done thing. Loss is consuming, then it recedes, and there is relief until it comes around again. Find your joys in your relationships in the world, and let the joy become you. You are not meant to suffer in this world. You are meant to accept your lessons and keep afloat with the support of the spirit world to ease your pain, suffering, or discomfort and give you strength to share your love and light with others.

Questions to ask yourself:

- What does your heart desire?
- What activity or project is on your mind when you wake up each morning?
- What do you catch yourself daydreaming about?
- Does it make you feel happy or sad?
- Does it give you strength or drain you?
- Does it add lightness or create fear?

- Does it make you smile or create anxiety?
- What is my value?
- What do I believe I can accomplish?
- What does the future hold for me?
- What is my benefit to others?
- What is inside of me that needs expression?
- What is my heart saying?
- What obstacles would prevent me from moving forward with this dream?
- Can I put my fear aside and make it a reality?
- Can I allow myself the freedom to express my desires?
- What steps can I take today to help myself step into this new venture?

Soulful Notes

SECTION 4

Mystical, Magical, Mindful Moments

"Signs from our loved ones in spirit are a reminder to us of the magical quality of how the spirit world intersects with our life in uplifting, mystical, magical, mindful moments and messages."

—**Nancy Yuskaitis**

When you are smiling, your loved ones are celebrating on the other side and cheering you on.

Signs from your loved ones in heaven are everywhere and are designed to offer comfort, encouragement, and support during times of grieving. They can also show up when preparing meals, at family gatherings, birthdays, anniversaries, in emotional distress, health challenges, travel, and at any time you could use a reason to smile or a reminder of your loved ones' continued presence in your life.

They are anxious to send you a message that all is well in their world. Let yourself become more attuned to your surroundings. Be mindful of the awe-inspiring beauty to be found in your daily activities that are being sent to you in sights, sounds, and scenes in nature.

The spirit world never ceases to amaze me in sending uplifting signs to us. Some are subtle, and others are "crystal clear" in how they fit into your life at the perfect timing.

Spirit signs can show up in beautiful ways to catch your attention and bring you back to the present moment, as well as to provide confirmation and reassurance that you may be seeking in your life. They appear with love to remind you that you are not alone while providing love, light, peace, and goodness in your world.

Receiving a sign is also a direct message from your loved one with the intention to let you know that all is well in their world. It can express how they now take great pleasure in caring for your well-being. By allowing yourself to become more attuned to your surroundings and mindful of the unexpected beauty in your daily activities, you will discover sights, sounds, and scenes that are direct signs from heaven. You may ask your loved one or the universe to send you a sign that you will undeniably recognize as confirmation that is particularly beneficial and healing to you.

Giving yourself permission to receive these signs and messages is an important part of the process, as well as asking for a sign that is helpful and recognizable to you. Some of these occurrences may happen so often that you will recognize them as signs, but others seem to come out of the blue with unexpected confirmation of their presence with you.

Twenty
Waiting for the Rainbow

"Confirmation that your loved one is still with you as you transform, heal, and grow is a profound experience and one that leads to a greater understanding of the fullness of life on earth and in the heavenly realms."

—*Nancy Yuskaitis*

Asking for signs was important to my well-being, especially from my Soulful Starlights, so that I could be reassured of my ability to survive this physical separation and loss with magical moments and messages of hope and promise.

In my grief, I was reminded through these signs of being guided and protected by my daughters in the afterworld that our heart-to-heart, soul-to-soul connection remained. The relief that I was not alone in my grief with each sign allowed me the opportunity to experience the grace and love that helped me to keep going.

I always give abundant thanks to my daughters and to the spirit world, even as I sometimes wipe a tear from my cheek or smile in delight. Your loved one may be trying many things to get your attention, and you never quite know when a sign will appear, so pay attention and don't forget to say thank you. It will mean the world to them and to you to connect again heart-to-heart, soul-to-soul.

I wish for you the awareness of the beautiful signs that your loved ones in spirit are sending you with their love and encouragement to live life to the fullest. Remember, all you need to do is ask the spirit world, your angels, guides, or loved ones to provide a sign that you will recognize and that brings peace and comfort in knowing their presence is with you. I am told by the spirit world that giving your permission to receive signs is very important.

You may ask while in meditation, before you drift off to sleep at night, or when in nature, where you can be aware of what you see, hear, or experience. It will amaze and delight you, I promise. You can also ask a medium to assist you in asking for signs to be aware of while receiving the confirmation you desire in your healing process. Some signs may appear to you repeatedly, as some have for me, and others may only happen once but be so awe-inspiring you won't forget them.

Since 2016, the signs I've received have been abundant and diverse and have nurtured, surprised, and amazed me with each one. I will share some with you that range from quietly beautiful to very, very obvious in getting my attention. Most of these examples are from my daughter, Crystal, and it may be that she sends them more frequently or because they are bolder, just like her personality, so they can't be missed.

These signs are called "Mystical Magical Mindful Moments," and they can take place anywhere, so stay mindful and aware of your environment and surroundings. Many signs I've received have been in nature, such as giant feather clouds and flowers that seem to just drop from the sky at the right moment to be comforting and healing. Other times, I've been blown away by initials and names in candles, coffee cups, and casino winnings.

Are you inspired to receive heartfelt signs from your loved ones in spirit? Now is the time to directly ask for one that is easily recognized by you and to stay aware of sights, scenes, and sounds around you for them to be revealed.

DREAMS offer the experience of the magical mixed with reality and are a wonderful way to experience a visit or conversation with a loved one that can bring about peace and healing to your grieving soul. Often, they are filled with adventures and travel, engaging with others you may or may not have met before. While you are sleeping or in that in-between state between dreaming and being awake, it is a perfect time to experience a visit, have a conversation, or receive a hug or sign from your loved one that will bring peace to your grieving heart.

In my dream state, my daughters would work alongside my guardian angels to provide healing treatments to lighten my heavy grief, increase my well-being, and restore my energy to allow joy to return to my heart. These sessions were extremely nurturing and restorative and had immediate and long-lasting beneficial effects. Sometimes, when I am in that in-between state between dreams and wakefulness, I can feel my Starlight's presence with me. I can see us hugging, with my hand on the back of Crystal's curly hair, as our cheeks touch in greeting. I can also see Lavender, with her long, dark hair, standing smiling alongside her.

Dream: Rehab in Heaven

I awoke in tears on the morning of our nineteenth wedding anniversary, just four months after Crystal's departure from this life. In the early hours, just before rising, I had a beautiful, heartwarming, and completely authentic dream where I visited with Crystal. In this dream, I was sitting around a table with a group of writers when one of them said, "I need to show you something." We walked outside and stood in front of a beautiful, large, ornate building that appeared to be a historic hotel and meeting place. As I stepped inside, I noticed, to the right, in the vast open room, rows of cots with bright blue coverings and a large group of people seated together, talking amongst themselves. I scanned the faces of those seated, and to my surprise, I came across my daughter's face. She noticed me at that same time; her eyes brightened, and her face lit up, and I could see her light brown curly hair bouncing as she floated toward me.

We excitedly stood together as she asked, "Have you come for me?"

We embraced in a deep hug, and I said, "Yes," although I was bewildered that I was even there by her side.

"Can I go with you?" she requests.

Oh, I don't know if you are ready to be able to leave for a visit yet, I curiously state. Let's call and ask Bob, she says.

"Bob, can Crystal come home for a visit?"

Yes, bring her home he answers. We both smile with excitement and then she returns to her seat at the back of the group, which seems like a counseling session at a rehab in heaven. Oh, what a wonderful dream, if only she could have come home with me in her physical body that day. Thankfully, I feel the warmth of her presence with me on many days.

Mom, I am here. I'm still here with you. Do not feel like I have left you. You are and will always be important to me, and I will watch over and comfort you every day of your life, just as Lavender has done previously. You are in good hands, trust me. I know I let you down so many times in my life, but everything has changed, and I am a different yet similar person now that I have crossed over to the immense world of love & light. There is wisdom here, compassion, and so much light and love to share with the world. You will be amazed when it's your time to come into the light of this magical world, but in the meantime, you're welcome to visit me here whenever you'd like. I know you have already stopped by to see me when I was sitting in a large group in one of the circles of loving guidance in heaven. Let life flow through you, let your emotions come and go, and try not to get caught up in the painful ones. All emotions are good, and some are beautiful, while others are agonizing. However, the goal is to experience life in all its ups and downs, including both its good times and grief-filled ones, without letting them knock you down and take the wind out of you. I know you miss me and always will, and I get that. I wish it didn't have to hurt so bad. I feel protective of you when you cry, and I am right by your side when you call my name.

Meditation

As you begin meditating, you will find that there are places you go, scenes that captivate you, and experiences you encounter that are beneficial to your well-being and state of mind. For myself, it has always been a beach with soft white sand and palm trees. For you, it may be a mountaintop, a flower meadow, a garden in the city, or your own backyard.

As you sit in the quiet listening to the sound of your breath, it provides an avenue to be at peace and to feel your loved one's presence, which may offer a message or sign that brings guidance and reassurance that is of helpful value. Combining this with journaling will help you remember any messages or guidance you receive from your loved ones or angels and guides.

Nature

Sitting by the ocean, mountain, river, or stream, wherever you feel most at peace, offers the time and place to receive a sign, message, or feel your loved one with you.

In a dream, let your loved ones, angels, and spirit guides go with you into nature to more fully encompass the beauty that surrounds you. At the beach where dolphins play, you will discover lighthearted expression to be yourself, to let go of any restrictions that hold you back from being an inspired, empowered, loving, and joyful soul. On a hiking trail with a stunning mountain view, you may recognize your courage, connection with nature, and the peace within. On the wing of an airplane, you will discover the magical beauty of your world as you soar above the clouds. Let yourself ride so high that you meet with your loved one in the spirit world. Listen to them express to you your strength and courage and feel certain of the support available to you from them.

You may or may not be surprised to realize that when you are in nature, there are spirit guides who join you. In meditation, one day I met a personal Zen master, Bright Eyes, who brings with him a sense of calmness that permeates the space around him with peace. This energy allows the opportunity to tune into the minute experiences going on in the natural world around you, in the humming of a bird, a bunny hopping by, a bee sipping nectar, or a butterfly landing nearby. This focus can take you away from your grief for a moment of restoration and healing that can soothe your soul and increase your well-being.

Soulful Starlight Message

I invite you to take a moment to slowly inhale and exhale a few deep breaths to center yourself before beginning the following prayer. It is important to separate yourself from the outer world and focus on your inner light.

"Dear Spirit World, Angels, Guides, and Loved Ones, May the messages I receive today be of the highest intention for healing my heart, spirit, and soul as I move forward in this life with love, grace, and joy."

Ask your guardian angel to kindly bring forward a spirit from the other side who may have a message for you. Sometimes, there is someone who is urgently anxious to give you a message, apology, or comfort. This can be as brief as a word, a sentence, or as long as a letter. It can be loved ones, people from your past, or even famous people. As you visit with this spirit, you may sit next to them, stand in front of each other, or go for a walk. Allow them to impart a special message to you, offering peace, guidance, or confirmation of their continued presence in your life. In the end, be sure to thank the spirit world for any gifts, blessings, and messages you receive in love and light.

As an example, one day when I practiced this exercise, the messages I received were in the form of gifts, soulfully inspired adventures, if you will, that embodied the essence of my loved ones, such as a large basket of fruit from my maternal grandfather to symbolize the importance of abundance, generosity, and graciousness in welcoming friends and family in your home and life as he so often did in my childhood. My two daughters presented me with a nature-inspired adventure in the form of a large flower bouquet to symbolize their love and admiration for being their mother, the best mother they could have asked for, and a reminder to appreciate the blessings of my son and my granddaughter, who is a brilliantly bright, soulful little girl. A rose quartz heart was placed within my heart, providing healing energy to my grieving heart that I could come back to and charge by placing my hands over my heart. In your meditation experience, you may receive a symbol such as a world globe to symbolize your empathy, care, and love for the planet and those around the world, or you may be given a Buddha statue symbolizing the gift of peace to your heart and soul in a Zen-inspired adventure. A crystal ball in sparkling blue was once handed to me in meditation to impart my intentions for my life moving forward in collaboration with my daughter, Crystal.

Music Messages

Songs provide the spirit world with the opportunity to express to you the exact words you may need to hear at the perfect time to confirm your loved one's presence in an attempt to uplift, comfort, apologize, or share love. Hearing special verses that just seem meant for you at the perfect moment can provoke a powerful emotional response that is overwhelming as you feel the intensity coming through the sound waves.

The words "Mama, I'm flying," as in the song *No Other Love* by Chuck Prophet or *Hello* by Adele, saying, "Hello from the Other Side," can come out of nowhere and be quite emotional for me, yet provide immense healing. Michael Franti's music was very uplifting and had me dancing alone in the kitchen on many days. Robert Earl Keen's song *Feeling Good Again* touched my heart in hopeful ways each time I heard it. If you are open to it and can allow it, music can be a very powerful healing balm. *No Roots* by Alice Merton always reminds me that Crystal is by my side, and when I hear it, I turn up the volume. It was written with the inspiration of feeling like there is no one place to call home, but having a home with people you love, and she definitely lived that lifestyle.

Twenty One
Spirit Signs and Scenes

"Sometimes, you need a rainbow to appear as a sign to let you know that all is well in your world. Rainbows are signs that bring hope wrapped in colorful blessings."

—*Nancy Yuskaitis*

Signs from spirit offer a connection point between our two worlds that can provide the opportunity to experience immense peace, beauty, and comfort in our daily life. I found it's important in a healing journey to write about these experiences in a journal as well as to capture a photo that brings about a positive memory whenever you view it.

Pink Roses in Memory

Roses are a favorite flower of mine that played a wonderful role in healing my grieving heart while soothing my soul. When Crystal left our world, I received a few bouquets of flowers and immediately felt a connection to the pink roses. So much so that I felt called to bring home a bouquet of pink roses each week in memory of her for over one year. Our connection from different worlds still felt strong, along with my longing for her presence, and in my attempt to feel closer to her, I used our love of flowers as a comforting gesture exchanged between mother and daughter.

I could feel a healing stream of energy directly from the spirit world to me through these roses. After some time, I included my Lavender in the experience, and it allowed me the presence of mind to grieve both of my daughters at the same time as I felt they were together now. I felt so strongly about doing this as a gesture in memory of my daughters that I could even feel their presence with me in the flower section of the store, helping me to choose the perfect bouquets to bring home. One for each of them. I noticed that the rose fragrance was comforting, the soft pink color emanated compassion, and the smooth texture of the petals felt soothing on my cheeks as I leaned in close.

Each morning, I would greet the bouquet of pink roses, speak silently to my late daughters, and breathe in the beautiful scent and healing energy of the velvet-like petals. This experience taught me to be mindful of the continuing connection with nature, which offers comfort in my overwhelming grief.

In fact, when we moved away from our cottage by the sea, a place that Crystal called home, my husband and I had a little ceremony on the eve before leaving where we sprinkled a little of her ashes along with the dried pink rose petals into the turquoise sea and watched them drift away setting her free in the water where she loved to swim. Although it's been some years since that time, whenever I encounter a pink rose, it takes me back to those treasured memories and poignant times in my life. Do you have a certain flower that reminds you of a loved one in heaven or possibly a sign that they are still with you?

Yellow Jeep Sightings

On a summer day, one week after the eighth anniversary of Crystal's passing, we left our home in Santa Fe, New Mexico, in our RV to explore a ski town a few hours away. Just before we walked out the door, I walked into my studio/office and quickly pressed a kiss on the Tiffany blue box containing her ashes that sat on a bookshelf containing treasures of hers or in memory in a little grief altar and asked her to accompany us on this trip. Talking to her in that room and hugging or leaving a kiss on her box is something I often do as a way of saying hello, goodbye, or goodnight. Within minutes of leaving home, she did, in fact, show us that she was indeed with us by having a yellow Jeep cross immediately in front of us in traffic not once but several times on our way to Red River. On the days that followed of that trip, yellow Jeeps kept showing up and crossing in front of us even as we walked around the small mountain town. Sometimes, we would be the only car on the road, and all of a sudden, a yellow Jeep would appear and pass us by.

While on that camping trip, I had a dream in which my daughter showed me a yellow Jeep. I heard myself say that if I found a toy yellow Jeep somewhere, I would buy it and take it with us. The next morning, my husband and I talked at breakfast and agreed to stay and enjoy the riverside campsite all day. About an hour later, he changed his mind and asked if I would want to go to town for lunch. I quickly agreed, as

Hi Mom, It's Me

I loved the idea of seeing more of Red River before leaving for home the next day.

We conveniently rode the shuttle bus to the restaurant and enjoyed a wonderful lunch before stopping in a few unique gift shops. I couldn't believe it, but the first shop we stopped in had an entire shelf of toy vehicles four to five inches in size, and standing there among the red and blue trucks was a couple of yellow Jeeps. Delightedly, I chose one because of my dream and because yellow Jeeps are a consistent sign I have received from Crystal since her sudden passing. It's an almost daily reminder to my grieving heart that my daughter is with me wherever I go. When we arrived home with the yellow Jeep, I set it on a shelf where I would walk by it often, but soon, my husband decided to place it prominently on the coffee table.

Within a few days, I felt called to move it back to the shelf by the front door and securely place it down. A little while later, I heard a crash in the entryway and discovered the Jeep had launched off the shelf onto the floor. As I picked it up, I could hear Crystal say, *"Hi, Mom, it's me."*

She stated she was trying to get my attention to offer assistance for our nine-and-a-half-year-old yellow lab, who had been sick for a few days. She had bonded with our dog when we brought her home at eight weeks and just loved her. She advised me to look up a condition involving dogs that ingested grapes, as it could harm their kidneys. This was helpful because our dog would seek out the ripe plums that would occasionally fall onto the backyard from the large tree out front. Her message alerted us to be more diligent in watching for these random plums and in removing them before Autumn could ingest them. Within a short time, Autumn was doing well again.

Yellow Jeep sightings began appearing that first week of my grief journey, as one I had never seen before started riding by our home on a very quiet street in our small mountain village. Each time it would pass by, its presence just called to mind my daughter and that she was close by watching over me and to feel that each time I encountered a yellow Jeep. Throughout the following years, yellow Jeeps have presented themselves in so many places I go that it is uncanny.

No matter the destination, whether it's a beach, an appointment, my granddaughter's preschool, or an art boutique, when I arrive, a yellow Jeep is already there waiting. When I go downtown for a concert, or a car show, or out for ice cream with my husband or granddaughter, there is a yellow Jeep crossing our path or parked next to us when I return to my car. While I am out with my family or running errands alone, there is always a yellow Jeep along the way. When friends of ours who were former neighbors in the Florida Keys bought a new vehicle, she posted a few photos, and I was stunned to notice it was a yellow Jeep. I promised to share this story with her as she and her wife knew Crystal.

Earlier this year, I was at a state fair with my son and his family, and the only vehicle parked inside the fair was a yellow Jeep sitting remarkably amid it all. A friend even gifted me a miniature yellow Jeep from an art show in Santa Fe that I treasure as a reminder of her and also Crystal. In fact, I get so excited that my granddaughter thinks yellow is my favorite color, even though she knows it's really blue. The variety of yellow Jeeps Crystal sends is amazing because they do show up in all sizes and styles, and many have interesting, colorful accents, like a huge array of little plastic ducks, a road runner, or a rooster tag or tire cover with words to bring extra delight and confirmation.

Jets: Crested Butte

During our many years of living in the Florida Keys, we would occasionally observe the large, loud military jets flying overhead. I found it interesting that each time I would be driving en route to visit Crystal, one would fly across the highway in front of me or over my car. It became a familiar sight on those days when I would spend time with my daughter, and I thought it was a consistent and interesting pattern of events. One week after Crystal's passing, I heard a booming loud engine flying overhead our home in the high mountains of Crested Butte, Colorado. Unbelievably, when I looked up, it was a military jet, just like I had seen all those times in Florida. This was the first time I ever noticed one fly over this little mountain village where we lived for many years, and it brought tears, knowing it was a sign from my daughter. She was checking in and saying that everything was going to be okay. My sadness was still overwhelming, and I could barely see the large jet through the tears, but I felt comfort in feeling her presence in a sign I would definitely recognize as hers. Only once more in that first month did I receive another sighting of a military jet flying over our home.

Uplifted and Nurtured

During the first summer of grieving Crystal's departure, I intuitively felt prompted to arrange for a visit to my favorite esthetician in Crested Butte, Colorado. This experience was nothing like any I've experienced before, and it was immensely comforting. It literally felt as nurturing as if Crystal was working through her hands on me while I received my facial. I had never felt so cared for in my life as I did in my relaxed state. I could hear her expressing to me, while she poured healing energy into my being that she was sorry she didn't cherish me more while she was alive, and now it's her turn to do so. After this experience, a calm and blissful state remained for the following twenty-four hours.

First Spirit Sign: Crested Butte

A few weeks after Crystal's departure, I awoke in Crested Butte in the early morning hours to witness a gigantic bright white feather cloud draped across the brilliant blue sky. It rose about 30 feet in the air and arched across the horizon. It filled the openness of our mountain view with a message from my girls so strong that I knew it was meant for me, offering peace and comfort in my sorrow.

Wish Pearl Necklace

The month after Crystal's passing, I was curled up in my upstairs bedroom, my heart feeling shattered and numb. I was doing my best not to shut down totally in self-defense, but hope was elusive to me at that moment. Suddenly, I looked up and noticed a pretty box nestled in between a stack of books standing on our bookshelf. As I reached for it, I soon realized that it was a birthday gift from Crystal that I had unwrapped but then placed on that shelf in our bedroom for safekeeping.

As I lifted this special gift tenderly and opened the beautiful packaging, I uncovered a lovely pendant necklace, a pearl encased in a little silver basket. The gift included a card describing that it was like a pearl, and it was to remain within the shell box until it was opened by a very special person, and then it would reveal its unique beauty. This peach-colored pearl has the intention to increase health and well-being. So perfect. Again, I felt nurtured and cared for by my sentimental girl, and with tears, I held it in my hand, feeling closer to her while doing so.

Tenth of the Month

This day of the month is very significant to me, and I actually feel different on that day, as if our connection is closer and I feel Crystal's presence with me more emphatically.

The number 10 is often brought to my awareness, as well as 1010, and seeing those numbers brings a powerful feeling of connection attached to it. The following is written for my daughter, Crystal, as I was drafting a letter to her, and her response kindly follows it.

Dearest Crystal,

In the early hours of July 10, my life changed as you slipped away from us in a quiet departure. My heart was shattered into a million little pieces, and my soul ached for you. I don't know who I am, this new me without you. Life without you here will never be the same: the highs, the lows, the new beginnings filled with hope and promise, the second chances and renewals will never happen again. We miss the brightness of your blue eyes and wide smile and your big hugs. The sound of your laughter with enthusiasm is unmatched. Your light-filled personality, generosity, resilience, tenacity, charisma, protectiveness, and sense of humor will forever remain. Your passion for cooking was memorable, and your sentimentality was unsurpassed. Your ability to rise above your circumstances to bring love, kindness, and laughter to others was truly your gift.

Mom, I am sorry you are hurting.

I realize that each time the tenth of the month rolls around, you think of me, and I can feel closer to you than at other times. It seems that we are energetically linked, and yet, on that day, the link gets even closer, and you can feel my presence more acutely.

It is ok. I realize that you are so sad that I have left my life with you so soon and so suddenly. I am doing well, better than I could have imagined at any point in my life.

There is love here, in abundance and understanding, as well as respect toward each other for the evolved beings we are and for our individual roles that we have developed over time on earth and in this realm. My life here is bubbling with opportunities to participate for the good of an individual here or on earth. I have been schooled in preparation for assisting those who pass over in a similar manner as I did.

Celebration of Life

A Celebration of Life is a chance to bring loved ones together to honor someone who has recently passed with heartfelt acknowledgment of the important role they held in our lives. For many, it's a chance to pay respects and say goodbye in a way that is fitting and allows a sense of closure. Believing that your loved one is there with you to experience the funeral, viewing, burial, or mass in their honor is a touching experience that provides strength and support beyond the earthly realm. Sometimes, their presence is felt so strongly that it is undeniable. I will share with you how Crystal's celebration of life was planned with her assistance from the afterlife.

I was so grateful for the crystal-clear blue sky, sparkling sea, and beautiful beach gathering to celebrate her in Key West on that day as she tenderly watched in spirit.

In the days prior, she let me know she wanted to assist and lighten my grief. She even encouraged me to have stickers made with her own sentiments to give out that day.

Tell my loved ones I tried. I loved my family & friends, the ocean & life itself.

Live in a way that you can be proud of when you die.

Live with no regrets, meaning live life with gusto and enthusiasm, go for it ... whatever you want to do, to be, to experience.

Tell them I lived my life in the best way I knew how, and yes, I have regrets about not experiencing deep loving relationships with all my immediate family, but just know you were always in my heart and thoughts. I never for a minute forgot about you all. I was just too embarrassed and humiliated to be around you. I lived with so much shame and self-judgment, and I was too vulnerable to be able to accept any more judgment from the family, who I let down repeatedly by my addiction and decisions. I was very conflicted most of my life by needing to be loved and accepted by my family, yet when I did the crazy things I did, the consequences pushed us apart.

I just want my family to know I loved them with all my heart and never meant to cause anyone pain. Remember me with love and laughter, silliness and smiles, good times, and hard-fought lessons learned. Life is short. Keep your dreams alive.

I am here, the same loving, happy being I have always been, and I am watching over you all in protective love.

Additionally, she had a few more things to say.

Don't let your limitations prevent you from achieving your dreams. Don't let life get in the way and stall what you are here to do in this life. Let yourself be free from burdens and things in life that weigh you down or cause you to not think highly of yourself.

After the ceremony, she offered a genuine thank you.

Mom,

I love you. What a beautiful, touching, emotional celebration you organized for me. I am in heaven, but you know I felt so loved and cherished all week by the intention and beauty and coming together of family on my behalf, it was just amazing. Every detail was beautiful and blew me away. Your heartfelt words made me cry, as I know I put you through so much over the years. Yet, our love for each other rose above all the hurt, turmoil, and despair that may have been experienced by each of us.

I always longed for you to be proud of me. It hurt me to always let you down in all the ways I did. Quite the rollercoaster we lived, you and I. Whew, I am glad that part of my life is over. I live in peace now, surrounded by beauty and loved ones, children and pets and my life now feels good. I am smiling all the time. You know, I tried to make my life on earth work for me, but I really didn't have the tools to succeed. Somehow, I came into life without some of the necessary skills needed to thrive. I know you always tried to give them to me, but I couldn't fully grasp them.

It's okay now. I will always be watching over you, guiding you, and sending love, peace, and blessings, just as you have for me all these years. You were so strong for my celebration; I was proud of you. You stood tall and talked to family and to me with dignity, grace, and courage. We were all impressed with your expression, passion, and creativity.

My day was so special from morning to end, and I enjoyed every minute of it. The prayer by my counselor, the testimony by an advisor, my stepdad's funny story, my step-brother's enthusiasm, and your young grandson's heartfelt words touched my heart. I was elated and truly on cloud nine. Your experience in the morning with the women in our family was special, and I loved the flowers and coastal decorations. What a bonding experience for you and for me to watch.

Everything you did expressed your passion to let me know how much I was loved and missed, and it was all amazing. Truly amazing, and I am so grateful for the beautiful way our family said goodbye.

I observed how emotional the flower toss was for you, and I saw you crying. It was so touching to watch each person I loved toss a pretty flower into the ocean in my memory. What a blessed event to encourage all to participate in. Wasn't that day stunning? It was a perfect sparkling sea kind of day, sunny with an ocean breeze.

Thank you for gifting me with such a wonderful surprise and lovely send-off. It was a remarkable experience that I will always cherish. I so enjoyed watching everyone all week, the fishing, you know how I loved fishing off your dock. The food looked amazing. I would have been in that kitchen, and you wouldn't have had to work so hard, but I could tell you were doing a great job. I love the new fireplace. It is so sweet to watch the family enjoying it.

What a special event for all to enjoy being together ... and all because of me.

Black Butterfly: Little Torch Key

One day we brought home a vivid pink bougainvillea tree that we purchased in memory of Crystal for our front yard. As we walked by it later that day, I observed a beautiful black butterfly with bright blue spots sitting within the branches as a thank you. I've certainly never discovered a black butterfly at any other time and it was stunning.

Circle of Light: Road Trip to New Mexico

As we traveled to where my husband and I would find our next home, I looked out the passenger window to see a stunning sight in the sky. A large white circle surrounded by a larger circle of pink and gold was nestled in an array of clouds of blue, green, and purple in the most magical scene. It was just overflowing with love and light that I could see and feel as confirmation that we were on a magical journey.

Crystal's Name in Lights

On my brother and sister-in-law's first visit to Santa Fe, we made the decision one day to visit a local casino. Not being a gambler, I casually sat down at a random slot machine. After only playing a few tokens, the lights started flashing, and I realized I had just won seventy dollars at a Crystal Seven game, and her name began lighting up on the slot machine. Crystal Crystal Crystal. It was unexpected, exciting, and a definite sign that she was with us.

Double Rainbow after Hurricane

On September 10, 2017, the lower Keys received a direct hit by Hurricane Irma as a Category 4 storm with tropical force winds, rain, and storm surge, causing devastating widespread damage.

We nervously watched the news from a distance, staying in touch with neighbors during the weeks before residents were allowed back home to survey the damage. I was fearful that our windows had blown out and Crystal's box of ashes had been ripped out to sea.

Gratefully, all was well at our seaside cottage, and I believe Crystal was certainly watching over her longtime family home and all the cherished treasures contained inside. Upon our arrival home, we were graced with a beautiful double rainbow as a magical sign from spirit. A Crystal Miracle for which we were extremely grateful.

Mother's Day: Little Torch Key

At home one day in the Florida Keys, I was pleasantly surprised by a knock on the door. I opened it to discover one of our dear neighbors with a beautiful bouquet of orange roses embellished with a beautiful butterfly sticker on one of the leaves. Her thoughtful and kind gesture on Mother's Day was a gift that truly felt heaven-sent and inspired by my Soulful Starlights.

Restaurant Orders

There have been quite a few occasions where Crystal's presence was felt at our family events. One morning, as our family gathered from out of town, we enjoyed breakfast in Big Pine Key. Everyone chose the breakfast buffet, but when the waitress appeared with a serving of shrimp and grits that no one had ordered, I laughed as she stated that she distinctly heard someone order it. I knew it was Crystal joining us, and I just beamed. It was after all the anniversary of her celebration of life.

Later, at dinner on Cudjoe Key, a similar occurrence happened where the server was certain someone had ordered grouper bites, and when she brought it, no one at our table had ordered it. I burst out loud laughing, saying, "I guess Crystal has decided to join us tonight," and we all clinked our glasses in a toast. I could feel the warmth of her smile during our family dinner, where we were celebrating her half-sister's birthday.

August Beach Sunset

On a trip to Dunedin, Florida, to visit my children's half-sister and her family, we ventured out to the nearby Honeymoon Island State Park for a beach sunset, and wow, what a spectacular night it was. For over an hour, the sky transformed in shades from brilliant orange to gold, in saturated to soft shades of pink and lavender in a wonderful demonstration, seemingly heaven-sent from my daughters who so magically joined us from spirit. I couldn't have known at that time that I would soon be living near this beautiful beach after spontaneously selling our Florida Keys home to be closer to family.

A Raven Visit

There is something quite striking about having a morning wake-up call from a beautiful, large raven tapping at your windows, banging on the side of the house, pecking on the skylights, and even stomping on the roof to get your attention. As our dog, Autumn, and I walked outside on an early Santa Fe morning, a large black raven flew from the roof over our heads and into the clear blue sky. I'm grateful to have observed this spiritual messenger and to reflect on his message. "Be present to the gifts being sent by spirit in nature as you deepen your commitment to the spiritual arts and connect with your angels and guides in new ways."

Candle Lighting

The International Wave of Light candle-lighting event is designed to commemorate the lives of all children gone too soon. It is an online event where people from all over the world light a candle in memory of their child and do so in their own time zone, providing a wave of light that illuminates the world. On one of these occasions in the Florida

Keys, I prepared two candles, one in memory of each of my daughters, to burn brightly for a few hours. As I lit a candle for Crystal, I set my prayerful intention and then lit the other one for Lavender and said my prayer. Immediately afterward, I picked up my phone and snapped a quick photo to capture my two candles to share online for the event. When I pulled up the photo and looked at my phone, I was stunned to see a distinct initial "C" in the wax of the lit candle. It was unbelievable. I don't think I could duplicate it ever again. It was amazing! It definitely showed Crystal's sense of humor, ability to communicate from spirit, and soulful presence at this poignant event. I just placed my hands on my heart and said, smiling, "Thank you."

Initial in the Coffee Mug

The following year, we were in Santa Fe, New Mexico, for the International Wave of Light. It was morning, and I was sipping a latte while writing at home. Of course, I was thinking about my daughters, Lavender and Crystal. As I glanced down into my coffee mug, I was absolutely stunned to see the letter "C" sitting at the bottom of the lime green mug on top of the foamed milk. I was absolutely delighted and amazed by this unexpected gift and a sign of my daughters' continued love and presence in my life.

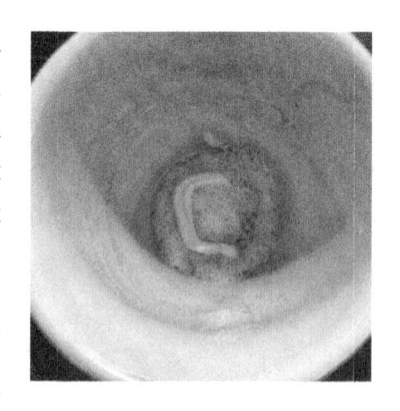

Christmas Bell

During Christmastime one year, I was working at home while experiencing a difficult time emotionally in grief, when suddenly, in the quiet of the afternoon, I heard a bell ring. I looked around and found nothing that prompted the sound, but as I looked further, I soon realized that it had come from our Christmas tree. A few years prior, on our anniversary, my husband and I had purchased little bell ornaments with our names written on them. It was the one stating "Nancy" that had begun ringing to get my attention. Within a few moments of being astounded, my guides let me know they had reminded me by "ringing my bell" with the message that I was not alone and that leaving a little bell out is a splendid idea for a signal to write and in that, I would receive comfort.

Healing from Beyond

As I was sitting in front of a crackling fire in our Florida home one evening this year, I felt my daughter, Crystal, place her hands on my shoulders to let me know that she is there supporting me as I traversed a health challenge, and she brought with her my mother in spirit. There has always been an awkward relationship between my mother and me from birth until after she left this world. I am aware that some parents just are not able to be present or nurturing and can be completely preoccupied with their own emotional needs, and it can have a long-term effect on the relationship.

Since my mother's passing in 2013, I have experienced several occasions where she would apologize to me through mediums or in my own automatic writing sessions. Still, the nurturing never came through to me until this time when my daughter brought her in as I was undergoing tests for a health condition that my mother experienced in her own life. Finally, I could feel my mother's genuine care and concern for my health, which prompted profound healing, allowing me to feel more at peace with our relationship and even offer a thank you to my mom and to my daughters for facilitating this healing on a deep level.

Pink Feather

On the community trail in our backyard is a little Zen garden I designed to offer a bright spot for those passing by. During the summertime, I leave an ongoing array of soulful kindness rocks for our neighbors to enjoy. At times, I have observed a butterfly, bunny, or raven stopping by to say hello. One morning, placed among the colorful stones, was a large, bright pink feather left there waiting for me. It was so unusual and a beautiful gift. I imagined it was from one of my angels who has pink wings, she lovingly wraps around me in protection and love.

2/26/25: Spiritual Assistance

The writing of this book was a challenge in the recurring reliving of my trauma of child loss, and it coincided with a bit of a health crisis. Each day was a lesson in determination and intense focus to work through the physical pain I felt from so many months of disturbed sleep due to pain. It was a similar type of pain I felt in my early grief, but I was being guided day and night to continue my efforts to manifest this book with the assurance of the spiritual support available to me.

In a high level of discomfort, I tried many things to relieve my suffering, including renewed intention for emotional release and soulful self-care, meditation, listening to my angels and guides, and looking inward. It became a constant plea from my soul to God and my spirit team to assist in clearing my energetic field and emotional and physical bodies from anything that no longer served or wasn't mine to carry in this healing work.

As we entered a new year and celebrated my birthday the following month, still in pain and discomfort, I asked for a message from my angels and guides to assist me in discovering what my body needed to return to wellness again. The answers came through an intuitive card reading. The messages I received may help anyone going through a challenging health or life situation.

"You can and will overcome this health situation in which you are currently living. Take special care of your being, rising above the situation with fortitude, strength, and awareness of your inner being.

Your spirit is feeling neglected in ways that are important to her. Go back to asking your spirit each day what she needs to feel comfortable, safe, and healthy. Your inner light is dimmed and needs to be reignited.

Ask Archangel Michael to help you with this, then allow this flicker to grow within you to nurture all aspects of your being. You will begin to notice improvements in your well-being after doing so. By taking time out, the answer will come through rest, restoration, recharging, and reflection. In your moments of rest, allow your body to rejuvenate to see the clearer picture that your body needs to heal. Allow yourself all the rest it needs. Be active and write daily again for guidance, assistance, and healing. You are going through a dark time with a rebirth coming. You are right to seek answers through medical consults for your pain and suffering, but also look within for answers too.

Your emotional body could use some attention. Positive self-talk is of great value now. You are brave, resilient, and strong. You are a warrior of love, light, and compassion. Your mindset is getting distracted with your pain and discomfort. Try your best to keep it on track. Trust your own counsel first. Use your intuition and the gifts you possess to access higher guidance to lead you to your next steps. You are blessed to have an open channel to the spirit realm. Don't keep it one-sided. We have much to share with you, as always. Keep moving forward, and don't let your fears of this book-writing process get in your way.

You can get well and work on your project at the same time; it's not one or the other. Many are accomplishing goals while struggling with a health crisis. Be assertive in your healthcare. By connecting with your soul, you do have what it takes to get through this health challenge. Promise to check in with yourself each day. You can be a pillar of strength and positivity. Be aware of the energies around you. They are filled with hope and resiliency. Allow your being to rest and recharge, but come back strong, vibrant, and filled with enthusiasm and ideas for your book. Asking for help is good but accessing the guidance in a written form is beneficial. Again and again, the message is to listen to your spirit team in automatic, intuitive writing, again. Keep your eye on your goal and your energy every moment. Regain your excitement for life and your author's life again. You must coach yourself now to assist you."

—Your Spiritual Guidance Team

Each step of holistic and traditional medical care I received was kind and caring in wonderful ways. I felt I was in good hands and exquisitely taken care of, and I appreciated the mystical and magical message I received as I turned into our neighborhood following a doctor's appointment one day when I heard the words of a song on the radio, "I am not alone, I see you everywhere in everything." I heard Crystal's voice in my mind immediately as a yellow Jeep passed by me, a definite sign of her presence.

Mom, we're here with you. We've got your back. You are never alone in your pain, physical or emotional.

Twenty Two
Meditation & Soulful Intuitive Writing

"Let yourself be drawn within to seek the answers your soul carries for you."

—*Nancy Yuskaitis*

The partnership of meditation and writing beyond loss provides a glimpse into greater awareness of your soul, encouraging you to look within for guidance, direction, and a new perception. It offers a different opportunity to step into the unlimited knowledge available to you with an openness to experience your soul's desires.

- Discover Clarity
- Awaken Creativity
- Release Grief
- Experience Peace
- Charge your Energy
- Listen to Your Intuition
- Meet Your Spirit Team
- Find Forgiveness
- Improve Wellness
- Uplift Your Soul

- Cultivate Joy
- Restore Renew Replenish
- Give Compassion
- Ignite Your Inner Light
- Connect with Loved Ones
- Accept an Apology
- Uncover Your Purpose
- Self-Nurture

Meditative writing saved my life. It gave words to the pain and allowed the process of healing from trauma to unfold. Whenever I needed to process or express an emotional space I was in or to receive clarity from the universe over a troubling experience, I found the nearest paper and pen and wrote about it. I was never quite sure what would be said or what I would be led to express or heal, but it kept me moving forward in life, in creativity, spirituality, and in my grief journey, feeling clearer, stronger, more supported, and abundantly hopeful.

Each time I was able to express myself in words on paper, a positive change occurred in my emotional state of being and in my heart. In times of crisis, creativity, or calm, writing has played a crucial role in living a more fulfilled life. It has been life-changing in that it has helped me to tap into my soul's purpose, receive insights from my guidance team, and connect deeply with my two daughters and other loved ones in spirit. Beyond that, it has inspired my passion to assist others on this journey beyond loss.

At this time in your life, as you strive to heal from traumatic loss, it is very important to be expressive in ways that feel helpful to you. I encourage you to sit down with your journal as often as you can to let your heart express what it needs to heal. Let it all out. Let your emotions pour onto the page as they come; don't censor them or block their expression. Let your emotions direct its tone and depth. If desired, ask the spirit world to share with you something that is helpful for you to know or understand at this very moment, and take a pause to listen as you write.

Meditation & Soulful Intuitive Writing

Combining journaling with meditation and your favorite oracle card deck can be another step to assist you in accessing the wisdom of your soul, your higher self, and your spiritual team in the higher realms who are available to co-create with you.

Steps to Begin:

- Choose a journal and a pen that feels inspiring and creative to you.
- Pick an oracle or inspirational card deck that you find beautiful or have an intention ready.
- Set aside at least thirty minutes of quiet time by yourself, if possible.
- Use your breath to calm and center yourself.
- Practice one of the many meditations provided in this book to go within.
- Set your intention for this session, its purpose, and desired benefit.
- Say an opening prayer, asking for your guardian angels to come close.
- Ask for blessings of protection and to receive the wisdom most needed at this time.
- Shuffle your deck and cut the deck in half. Choose three, five, or seven cards from the top.
- Lay these cards out in front of you. One by one, hold each card and observe its design.
- If there is writing on it, ponder its meaning in your life.
- As you hold a card, ask that its message for you becomes "crystal clear."
- Close your eyes, open your heart, and visualize the space around your head being open to receive.
- Ask your soul, guardian angels, or spirit team to provide the guidance you seek at this moment.
- Begin to listen to the intuitive thoughts that come into your awareness.

An Alternate Exercise:
- Breathe to calm and center yourself.
- Close your eyes and set your intention. Ask your angels, guides, and loved ones to join you.
- Say an opening prayer requesting that you receive the best message for yourself at this time.
- Open your eyes and pick up your pen and journal.
- Begin writing what's on your mind and keep writing until you feel your message feels complete.
- If nothing comes, write about what would help you to find comfort in your heart.
- Write about the soulful, inspired adventures you've experienced recently and how they impacted you.
- Developing a writing routine will help to set this practice in motion.

Allow these messages to speak to your heart and to provide solace and emotional support. As the words meant for you start to flow, let yourself write them down as quickly as you can. Keep writing for as long as the messages come with each card.

In the end, give thanks for the blessings of clarity, encouragement, and love you received. Thank your soul and the spirit world as you close this channel until the next time. Take some time to read your personal message or the impressions you received. Go forward believing in the transformative healing that just occurred.

Each day is a new and blessed gift to re-awaken to the guidance available to you. By allowing yourself to just be without preconceived notions, you will discover that you can listen to your higher self, soul, intuition, angels, guides, and loved ones. By allowing this opportunity of expanded awareness to be combined with a renewed sense of focus to be fully present, your guidance will be expressed to you for your highest well-being.

You can always return to these comforting and enlightening locations again and again to receive further benefits of wisdom, compassion, and healing. Imagine the experience of being transported to your favorite place on earth, one with immense beauty and peace, where you feel most radiantly alive and well. When you long to return to this healing place again in your meditation, you can easily do so.

Questions to ask yourself:

- Were you able to relax your mind?
- Did you observe any imagery in your journaling session?
- Did you receive any insights, awareness or messages?
- How do you plan to implement these in your life?

Soulful Notes

Let's do a little soulful self-care today. I invite you to take a few moments in meditation and/or journaling to check in with your heart and soul.

It's a simple process beginning with your breath. As you breathe in and out slowly a few times, you will feel yourself becoming calmer and more centered. In and out with your breath ... breathe in peace. Breathe out anything you wish to release at this time.

As you sit quietly, you may request your heart and soul to communicate with you as to its needs at this moment. It may involve a healing that affects you physically, emotionally, or energetically in ways that nurture your health and wellness.

Listen for any insights or impressions you receive that may assist in your journey to wholeness. At this time, feel free to express in writing any messages, guidance, or inspiration you may want to remember for later. The process of taking pen to paper after sitting in the stillness and peace of meditation can provide valuable insight into the state of emotions you are feeling and ways to nurture, uplift, and heal many areas of your life.

Sit comfortably, relax, and calmly breathe. Ask your guardian angel to come close and connect with your angel for protection and assistance. Set your intentions and be firm. Ground yourself and stay centered. Ask for a message for your highest good from a loved one, angel, or spirit guide. Begin this practice with a simple question. The more relaxed you are, the easier it is for you to receive a message. Allow them to speak to you in a way that you can understand. Take as many notes as you can, and always say thank you when you are finished. Then, ask your angel to end the session.

Meditation is a doorway to the highest potential. As you learn, you grow. As you experience, you change. As you lean in for guidance, all is revealed. As you ask for assistance, it is given in a timely way. As you live, you evolve all the days of this soulful life.

Depending on what you choose, you can determine the type of meditation to practice for your desired outcome. Each of us is given the opportunity to transform, heal, and grow within our lifespan. Let this be the time you begin to discover ways to feel lighter, more joyful, and intentional with awareness of your inner strength, wisdom, and beauty to transform your way of being.

Meditation & Soulful Intuitive Writing

You will discover new ways to feel uplifted with a magical glow that is transformative for your soul and your life by the use of meditation, intentional soul work, and soulful intuitive writing.

Questions to ask yourself:
- Imagine yourself entering this doorway or portal. What does it look like?
- Why does it intrigue you?
- How do you feel as you walk through it?
- Will you allow yourself to experience immersive healing in this place?
- Do you find yourself surrounded by certain colors that nurture you?

Soulful Notes

_____
_____
_____
_____
_____
_____
_____
_____
_____
_____
_____
_____
_____
_____

Sitting in the quiet stillness of meditation allows you an opportunity to be open to receiving a message or sign from family and friends more easily, especially if you can combine it with journaling to record anything you see, hear, or feel that is uplifting, healing, or comforting to you.

During *meditation*, is when I often see my two daughters, and we share a visit in a beautiful cottage or castle by the sea. We exchange warm greetings and big hugs and respond to each other in a loving, joyful manner. At times, we would walk hand-in-hand down the shoreline of a beautiful beach in the aquamarine waves, basking in the sunshine of being together. On one occasion in meditation, I requested to return to Heaven's Beach by the Hall of Records to visit with my "Soulful Starlights."

In my mind's eye, I see this beautiful beach lined with narrow chunks of gemstones in the sand like piano keys in shades of the rainbow, and the ocean is a brilliant blue. It was during my birthday month one year ago when my girls greeted me warmly with an abundance of gifts to support my emotional health in the coming year. The first gift was a large "pink quartz heart" that was placed inside mine, offering continued comfort and compassion. Next, I was given a "blue starfish" for creativity and spirit connection, a "pink dolphin" swam by providing delightful playfulness, and a "Pegasus white horse with wings" arrived, offering a lightness of spirit to remove heavy emotions and the ability to rise above situations when needed.

A "yellow butterfly" gave confirmation that I am never alone but supported with every step. A small tree was given to foster health in my body, mind, and spirit. A "blue book" was handed to me to record my highest dreams and desires, along with a "gold pen" to write spirit messages from the afterlife. Golden sunlight brightened the day, invigorating my being and nurturing my body while illuminating my soul. There was a "rainbow with wings," a movable reminder of moments of joy that capture miracles in everyday life. I was introduced to a "pink unicorn and a blue dragon," spirit guides who protect my energy and provide safety in shimmering love and light.

Meditation offers you the opportunity to relax your body, head to toe. As you sit or lie down, you may ask yourself what your intention is for this healing practice and then observe each emotion as it comes into your consciousness. As you do, visualize any dark, negative, or painful emotions rising to your awareness, dissipating one by one, and leaving your body.

There are many types and styles of meditation, from guided ones in a group, listening to one from an app on your phone, or using your own mantra, as well as some that include walking, expressive art, or intuitive writing. I found each one extremely helpful in releasing and softening my grief and letting go of what I may be carrying that is no longer necessary for my optimal health and well-being. Meditation is also a wonderful way to receive guidance from your soul, your guardian angels, and spirit guides, as well as from your loved ones who are waiting to assist.

Ask one of your spirit guides, angels, or loved ones to come into your awareness with gentleness to assist you in healing your emotional, spiritual, physical, or energetic levels and to surround you in light. Observe the intentions of your heart as you ask it to gently be receptive to the loving, compassionate guidance that is available to you. Allow your heart to soften as you breathe in your personal intention for this experience and ask that whatever you need to know at this moment is revealed to you. You may find yourself immersed in the healing energy that is emanating around you as you continue to breathe in your intentions and breathe out anything that no longer serves your highest good and is transmitted into light as it leaves your energy field.

You may also, at this time, tune into your soul and ask to be given or shown ways to heal and transcend as you move forward in uplifted living. Allow yourself to embrace the radiant healing energy from the universe as it infuses your body and soul with the power and magic of transformation.

Upon practicing the following meditations several times, I began to feel a noticeably improved sense of relief in the form of lessened physical and emotional pain along with increased comfort and healing as I let go and released my overwhelming grief, while at the same time allowing the light to brighten the dark places within my heart. As this occurred, my soul began to feel nurtured and loved with kindness and compassion beyond compare. Hope began showing up in my awareness of better days to come. Fleeting moments of peace arrived, ushering in greater moments of peace to follow. Life held the promise that I could survive devastating loss again.

Give yourself all the time you need to go through this process slowly with gentle kindness and intention, especially if this is your first time practicing meditation. Painful experiences and memories are stored with our bodies and must be released, especially if you are feeling an intense headache or back pain, a depleted spirit, and a heart that is partially closed. Extra sleep is often required in times of great release. It's best to pull away from social media and other unnecessary distractions during this delicate time. You are very open and somewhat vulnerable, so ease back into your daily life with gentleness. As you complete each session, breathe in peace, radiant healing light, and uplifting joy. Let it move through you, and let yourself be renewed and refreshed. It may require multiple sessions of quality, undisturbed time to feel your emotions and, one by one, release them from every part of your body where they have been stored, waiting to be released.

Questions to ask yourself:
- Have you allowed yourself time to center and calm your being?
- Do you prefer guided meditations or sitting in quiet stillness?
- When was the last time you practiced meditation, within the last week, month, or longer?
- Do you prefer to use a mantra or focus on your breath to achieve relaxation?
- Are there angels or spirit guides in place supporting you?
- What do you need to know at this moment in your life?
- Are there messages from your loved ones in spirit waiting for you?
- Do you need more peace, vitality, abundance, or joy in your life today?

Soulful Notes

Mini Meditation

- As you sit quietly, let yourself notice the emotions you are feeling at this moment.
- Are you feeling discomfort, pain, sadness, grief, anger, or regret?
- Acknowledge your feelings, for they are a valid response to your life at this moment.
- In a soulful self-care approach to healing, ask yourself to set the intention to breathe in peace with each inhale and to breathe out what no longer serves you in each exhale.
- As you repeat this exercise several times, visualize these emotions being released from your energy field and body.
- Allow yourself to breathe in and embrace the feelings of calmness, peace, and ease in your emotional body and throughout your being.
- Breathe in peace and comfort.

Cloud Meditation

- Imagine yourself floating up, up to where the clouds fly free.
- Big, billowy, soft clouds bouncing weightlessly.
- Let yourself choose one that looks comfy and safe.
- Gently lie down with your back resting comfortably in the softness.
- Notice how you feel buoyant and free.
- You have no concerns or pain. You are content and safe.
- Let yourself relax and rest in the open expanse of the sky.
- Breathe in the lightness and peace surrounding you.
- Allow any concerns, pain, grief, or sadness to drift away.
- Ask that any emotions that no longer serve you are released.
- Only peace and joy remain in your experience.
- Listen for messages you may receive from your angels or spirit guides.
- Take note of any observations you may take back with you.
- Allow lightness and freedom to go with you as you float back home.
- Ahhh, breathe in the peace, and so it is.

Daybreak by the Sea Meditation

Before you begin, it's helpful to set your intention to breathe in "peace" and, with each exhale, to breathe out "sorrow." As you begin your meditation, visualize the feeling of calming peace entering your body and filling your heart with contentment. As you breathe in this feeling of peace and contentment, let it swirl around your body and especially around your heart. In your exhale, visualize the heaviness of grief and sorrow being released from your energy field and body, drifting away and dissipating into the ocean to be transmitted into positive energy. Let yourself embrace the feelings of calmness, peace, and ease in your emotional body and throughout your being.

Variations: Breathe in harmony, wellness, acceptance, light, radiant health.

Breathe out: Fear, discomfort, pain, sadness, regret, despair, anger, illness, or disease.

- Breathe in all the good feelings that you wish to experience, such as love, joy, peace, wholeness, radiance, vitality, clarity, belonging, whatever comes to your awareness.
- This experience can provide a subtle release or a more dramatic one, but I promise you, your soul will feel lighter and more hopeful in the process.

Color Swirl Meditation

During the initial stages and first year, my heart physically ached with the pain of a thousand elephants sitting on my chest. It was imperative that I find techniques to relieve the pain and pressure I was feeling day and night. My ability to take a deep breath was affected, as was my physical body. I just wanted to keep my hand on my chest all the time to calm and comfort my grieving heart. After practicing this technique just a few times, I began to find relief in the way of lessened physical pain. With each session, I invited more light into my heart and being to heal, mend, and release the heaviness of grief. On certain days, I would vary the use of color inside the swirl of energy I would visualize. My entire body, mind, and spirit benefited from the letting go and release of grief in a daily practice of meditation. My physical and emotional body received comfort and healing as I imagined light filling the dark places within my heart. Fleeting moments of peace arrived, offering a welcome respite for my overwhelming sadness. Life held the promise that I could survive this devastating loss.

- Sit or lie down comfortably. Invoke a color of light of your choice.

- Golden white for cleansing, pink for love, green for renewal, or blue for clarity.
- Visualize this light entering the top of your head (crown chakra) from the universe.
- In your mind's eye, see it flow past your third eye and down to your throat chakra, bathing it in healing light.
- Let this light begin to swirl around your heart chakra in a spiral. With each spiral, inhale and hold for a few seconds, and exhale.
- Visualize this golden light filling your heart with love and compassion for yourself.
- With each turn, imagine your heavy grief being released from your body and spirit, allowing light to fill in and heal your brokenness.
- Let these painful emotions move through you.
- Keep breathing deeply. Don't allow yourself to focus on the pain.
- Let the hurt and sadness float away.
- See yourself being surrounded by a bubble of white light protecting you from fear or anxiety, allowing only peaceful, hopeful, and uplifting thoughts and feelings to radiate within you.

Angel Healing Meditation

In front of me was an immense rainbow waterfall. Each shade of the falling water was more vivid than the one before. The colors were fanned out, and each one would fall independently from the others. I gently waded into the perfectly refreshing waters to stand under the streaming energetic water as each shade of chakra colors flowed over me for the refreshment of my senses, rejuvenation of my spirit, and balancing of my energetic field.

I slowly stepped away from the waterfall and placed a soft, fluffy white robe over my shoulders on my way to a healing room located in a free-standing small adobe stone building nearby. Upon entering, I was greeted by my two Guardian Angels of Light, whom I am very familiar with, one with pale blue wings and the other with pale pink wings.

Each held a lit candle and beckoned me to lie down on a raised bed that was draped in white sheets; the walls were lightly painted, and the ceiling was very tall. It was very peaceful and calm.

As I gently rested, a feather was placed over my eyes, and a rose quartz was placed on my heart chakra. The room was then bathed in a blue healing light as my angel in blue waved his hands over me. There was a palpable feeling of him releasing areas of emotion that I was holding onto that were no longer beneficial to me. He waved a very large, silvery white feather over my body, starting at the top of my head, clearing with seven swipes from left to right.

As my male guardian Angel worked on me, he cleared away many long-held difficult emotions stored in my body, spirit, and soul. As he did so, I could feel my grip on those emotions loosen, and my palms opened in response. I consciously let them go in complete trust and openness, leaving me feeling fresher, free-er, and renewed.

He then stepped aside as my female Guardian Angel in pink came close to my side. Starting at the top of my head all the way to my feet, she sprinkled pink and gold glittery light onto my being. This light was filled with immense love, compassion, and solace. It was given to me to continue my healing going forward on a walkway of pink and gold shimmering light and love.

All the recently cleared spaces were filled with this lovely healing energy as she waved a large white feather over my body. Sparks of light like glitter and sparks of fire rose in the air around me. She then grazed the right cheek on my face with this feather to ignite my spirit with the ability to share this healing light with others moving forward.

As the session ended, I was led back to sit by the shore of the falling rainbow waterfall with the following message. You are a light being of the highest order. We cherish our guardianship over you and stand alongside you as you venture out into the deeper waters of life, expanding your outreach and impact on the world of beautiful souls in your care.

Crystal Mermaid Meditation

As I began to meditate, the Soulful Starlights encouraged me to join them at a little cottage by the sea. In my mind, I saw myself walking up to the cottage and entering through a cobalt-blue front door. Inside, there were wide open spaces filled with golden Reiki energy and light, flickering candles, and tables filled with fresh flowers and crystals.

As I stepped out of the large double door, it opened out to a wide expanse of ocean. I noticed a sitting area with a white U-shaped couch dotted with three pillows. One with "Peace," one with "Joy," and the other with "Light," written on them and a backdrop of shimmering turquoise blue curtains. Sitting on the beach was a large, bright yellow Adirondack chair with the words Enjoy the Moment painted on the back. The beach was lined with beautiful shells and colorful sea glass. The Soulful Starlights greeted me warmly, it felt real as day to be there with my daughters. The exuberance they exhibited was wonderful to see as they walked arm in arm, showing me around this little beach cottage. It was a remarkable experience to observe them playfully happy together as they never lived on earth at the same time, yet clearly were connected as sisters now in heaven.

On one side of the cottage, there was a rock path, and tropical fruit trees were growing next to an organic garden. By the sitting area, there was a tile-paved labyrinth with a round bench inside where my male Guardian Angel, Gabriel, was sitting. We shared a coconut drink and a slice of mango as we conversed. A bouquet of pink roses was extended to me by my daughters as a gesture to me for always dedicating pink roses to them in their memory. The feelings I could take away with me from this meditation were of love and a fresh new perspective about time here on earth and a message: *We are all given a moment to reflect on our service to others in this world. It is our generosity of spirit that beckons us to offer guidance and communication from the afterworld to loved ones still living on earth.*

Soulful Grief Meditation

The expansive doorway in front of me was adorned with vines of greenery, white twinkling lights, and strands of shimmering gold.

It was breathtaking.

Golden light beamed inside the doorway.

I was called to step inside.

Just one step into this golden space was all I needed that day.

The brilliant and energetic light showered me with healing.

Soon, I began to feel the pain, sadness, and grief that was being tightly held within my cells to be released.

I could visualize it dripping out of my body through my outstretched arms all the way to my fingertips.

This release of heavy emotions dissipated into the ethers.

I became aware that my heart felt uncomfortably closed.

I welcomed the golden light of peace and love to swirl around my chest and heart chakra as it relaxed, allowing the golden light to fill my heart space and restore my spirit.

As I basked in the glorious feeling of calm, I clasped my hands in Namaste and with a nod of gratitude, I walked out of the beautiful doorway with full awareness of my open invitation to return to this magical place of healing whenever I felt the need.

I stepped out into the clear blue starlit night, feeling transformed.

Soulful Healing Meditation

Are you open to receiving guidance and inspiration in ways to transcend your pain to peace?

- Sit or lie down comfortably.
- Imagine yourself entering a beautiful healing space. Visualize the doorway or portal you choose to walk through.
- Let your body be calm.
- Set your intention to allow the weight you are carrying to fall away.
- Let your mind quiet down.
- Let your breathing become consistent with an inhale and an exhale in a slow count of four seconds.
- Allow any stress, discomfort, anger, resentment, fear, sadness, or grief to come to your awareness.
- At this time, focus on one emotion you are feeling that is distressing you for this session.
- After you determine the one emotion that is most pressing, sit with it for a few moments.
- Acknowledge that it is a familiar emotion to you as you keep breathing consistently.
- Slowly, in your mind, allow your heart to open.
- Observe the fullness of your heart as you ask it to gently be receptive to the loving, compassionate, and supportive guidance that is available to you.

Let your heart soften as you breathe in your intention for this experience and ask that whatever you need to know at this moment is revealed to you.

You may allow yourself to become immersed in the healing energy that is emanating around you as you breathe in your intentions and ask that anything that no longer serves your highest good is released and transmitted into light as it leaves your energy field.

Let yourself embrace the radiant healing energy from the universe as it infuses your body and soul with the power and magic of transformation.

You may, at this time, tune into your soul and ask to be given or shown ways to heal and transcend as you move forward in uplifted living.

Ask one of your spirit guides, angels, or loved ones to come into your awareness with love to assist you in healing your emotional, spiritual, physical, or energetic bodies and to surround you in light.

At the end of this meditation, give thanks to God, the spirit world, and the universe for all that you have experienced or received as you walk through this doorway out into your world in a new, fresher way of being.

Take some time afterward to write down any messages, insights, or guidance you received while you are in this safe space of receptivity and growth.

SECTION 5

The Art of Soulful Inspired Living

"Living an inspired life consists of cultivating a mindful awareness of the simple beauty found in everyday experiences that bring uplifting joy."

—*Nancy Yuskaitis*

The Art of Soulful Inspired Living was created as a personal path to surviving child loss for the second time. In such a vulnerable state of mind, I wasn't quite sure how to go about navigating a healing journey, but I was certain I needed one. I began by observing and implementing experiences in my life that assisted in releasing the trauma and nourishing my body, heart, and soul in what I was inspired by the Soulful Starlights to call Soulful Inspired Adventures, using mindfulness and meditation in nature, creativity, writing, culinary art, and self-care.

In doing so, a process of healing began to restore a sense of purpose in my changed reality. Each new day, I sought to live consciously with mindful awareness of everything in my life that could provide uplifting comfort and healing in healthy ways. I found solace in daily walks, meditation, Reiki energy, the spirit realm, and connecting with my soul in new ways. I also observed that offering encouragement, compassion, and kindness to myself was nurturing in my sorrow and that by practicing intuitive writing, I could access the healing wisdom my spirit needed to integrate my grief and share this process with others.

A Soulful Inspired Adventure is designed to:

- Restore a sense of peace in a changed reality.
- Live consciously with mindful awareness.
- Provide compassion & kindness to yourself.
- Discover healing in the beauty of nature.
- Appreciate creative expression in music and art.
- Offer solace from the spirit world.

- Connect with your heart and soul in new ways.
- Express emotions and give words to the pain and grief.
- Reclaim joy in experiencing soulful inspired adventures.
- Inspire you to live life to the best of your ability.
- Recognize the uplifting signs and messages from the spirit.
- Expand your view and perspective on life and the afterlife.

Twenty Three
Mystical, Magical, and Mindful

"Let your grief soften and allow a feeling of joy to be experienced each day in uplifting and inspiring adventures in mindfulness."

—***Nancy Yuskaitis***

Soulful Adventuring is a transformative healing journey to living, loving, and reclaiming joy through mindful awareness and intention of our thoughts, feelings, emotions, and experiences and how they affect our quality of life, outlook, and attitude.

Soulful Adventuring is a mindset.

It is a spiritual adventure. An inspired life.

It is looking at our world in mystical, magical, and mindful moments.

It is about being conscious, listening to your intuition, connecting with your soul, and discovering ways to be peaceful, present, and purposeful while also experiencing gratitude, resilience, and joy.

It is about being fully present to the moment you are in as you are experiencing it, while being open to finding solace in your everyday experiences as a form of soulful self-care.

It is looking upon life through the ups and downs, the highs and lows, the love and loss, while believing through it all, you will not only survive but will be okay. You can reclaim peace, hope, and joy a little more each day through this practice. I personally know it's possible.

Observing the subtleties in life, along with the grand gestures, allows you the opportunity to appreciate the wonders of life up close in full detail, and on a big scale, including the seemingly minute occurrences that may simply go unnoticed.

There is a common phrase that adventure is good for the soul, yet when you have experienced loss, it seems vitally important to your well-being to find ways to uplift your heart and soul to:

Soulful Intentions:

- Live mindfully, one moment at a time.
- Savor the flavor of food and beverages.
- Discover ways to reclaim peace, hope, and joy.
- Appreciate the natural beauty of nature.
- Listen to your soul's intuition.
- Experience heartfelt moments of love.
- Move your body in healthful ways.
- Express in words and creativity.
- Find comfort in kindness and compassion.
- Infuse all the joy you can into each moment.
- Be nurtured in self-love and self-care.
- Recognize signs from the spirit world.
- Lighten up and enjoy one adventure at a time.

In my experience as a grieving mother and with the loss of each elder in the family, I became conscious of just how precious life is while being on a perpetual grief journey. Remembering the good times, working through the challenging ones, and discovering ways to enjoy life in mindful moments that our loved ones would appreciate keeps their personalities alive in our hearts and provides an opportunity to feel their presence alongside us in an activity so intensely that sometimes it brings tears of connection.

We each have the choice to seek healing, nurture our body, calm our emotions, receive inspiration, and reclaim joy with a compassionate heart, a courageous spirit, and an adventurous soul one moment at a time.

Soulful Adventuring

- It is taking the opportunity to observe the experiences that add value to our lives and to breathe in that uplifted state of being as we expand our awareness and tune into the desires of our hearts and souls.
- It is mindful intention with a generosity of spirit, compassion, empathy, and forgiveness for ourselves and others as we transform, change, and grow through loss and challenging life circumstances.
- Offers us the opportunity to discover healing in our own personal lifestyle, relationships, and activities that uplift and nurture our body, mind, and soul.
- It can raise our vibration and inspire us to reclaim joy if only we pause for a moment to soak in the feeling of being peaceful, loving, creative, hopeful, and kind each day.
- Observing the subtle beauty in our surroundings, as well as the grand gestures, allows the opportunity to value the wonders of life close up in full detail and on a broad scale.
- It is looking at life as an adventure to be experienced through the ups and downs, the highs and lows, the love and loss, while believing through it all, you will be okay.

- It is a healing journey to discover ways to uplift and care for your soul through mindful awareness, creative expression, and soulful self-care.
- It is being aware of the impact our activities, events, and adventures can have on our quality of life, outlook, and mindset.
- It is being mindful of the magic in nature, creativity, self-expression, a culinary experience, a travel destination, self-care practice, connection with a loved one, or any experience that nurtures your soul.
- It is an experience providing the possibility of hope that will broaden your state of mind, nurture your soul, uplift your spirit, delight your senses, open your heart, and expand your perspective with light-filled adventure and joy.
- Encourages soulful resilience, self-care, and taking chances on feeling happy again in the midst of loss and many other difficult life changes, challenges, and circumstances.
- It offers a way to see life through a magical lens where unexpected and delightful surprises can be found.

Scientists call these seemingly insignificant moments of pleasure that are experienced during simple everyday activities glimmers or sparks, offering positive short- and long-term responses in your body, mind, and spirit. Like glimmers, the benefits of soulful, inspired adventures happen when you consciously decide to focus on the beautiful and unexpected gifts of grace that are available to you as often as you can. Just the brief observation of these uplifting moments is helpful to your grief process, creativity, emotional resilience, and overall state of well-being.

I discovered through my Soulful Starlights that a way to live mindfully in the face of loss is to view life through a mystical and magical lens, where love and life continue on in the afterlife, in heaven, in a paradise in the sky.

Through this magical lens is where unexpected delight can be found in a chance meeting with someone who brings your loved one to mind in words, emotions or appearance or an extraordinary scene or occurrence in nature that gives you a feeling of gratitude for an experience that exquisitely feels heaven-sent.

It could be an exchange with another beautiful soul that is filled with immense love, compassion, and joy or a lively conversation with a neighbor, friend, or family member that brings uplifting comfort to your struggling soul and just feels as if your loved one is looking out for you. An opportunity may present itself where someone you have never met just randomly greets you with a special phrase or comment that catches you off guard and amazes you at the same time as a sign from your child or loved one.

I invite you to be mindful of the simple beauty and magic in your daily life, such as a beautiful butterfly floating nearby, a dolphin sighting, a bird's song, a bunny or deer stopping by for a visit, a favorite flower blooming in your garden, sky-watching the clouds of a sunset or sunrise over the mountains or the sea, expressing yourself in music, painting, photography or writing, a delicious libation or culinary experience, traveling to a new destination, a visit with cherished family or friends, a nurturing self-care activity or any other soulful inspired adventure that will clearly open your mind, nurture your spirit, fill your heart with joy, delight your senses and expand your horizons beyond your current life experience.

Soulful Suggestion

It takes being mindful at the moment to intuit what our state of mind is and what activity or situation could improve it. When you are grieving or feeling low, and life seems flat and colorless, it is helpful to take a step back and consider what your immediate needs are. In certain circumstances, it may be necessary to take a moment throughout the day to check in with yourself and to allow yourself to trust or provide that all your needs are being met for self-care and increased well-being.

Expand Your View

Love continues, as does life.
You are not alone in your life experience.
There is more than meets the eye.
It's the little things that matter, but not in the way you think.
Notice them up close, then expand the view.
Observe the subtitles in life, as they are more important than you know.
Take a closer look at the feathers of a bird or a flower petal,
then step back,
and expand your view to see the entire creature, garden, or tree.

Twenty Four
Soulful Inspired Adventures

"Soulful Reflections: The next step in her grief journey was to allow freshness, a glimpse of hope, and the possibility to seep into her grieving heart with light-filled, soulful, inspired adventures."

—*Nancy Yuskaitis*

Soulful Inspired Adventures are not just planned adventures, although they can be.

Many times, they are natural occurrences in our daily lives that often go unnoticed yet can provide uplifting healing to our body, mind, and soul.

Soulful Inspired Adventures combine various self-care practices, techniques, and adventures in mystical, magical, and mindful moments that can be found in the enjoyment of preparing dinner, dining out, listening to music, watching your favorite entertainment, being in nature, expressive art, spirituality, meditation, and heart-centered relationships.

They can be experienced everywhere, from the comfort of your home or at work, in scenic views and garden life, at sunrise or sunset, sitting in a café or taking an inspiring workshop, sitting at your kitchen table, or taking a walk around the block.

Soulful Inspired Adventures

For a mystical, magical, mindful moment, consider the following:
- *Cuisine* Inspired Adventure: An activity or experience providing a delicious journey into the world of culinary art and libations.
- *Nature* Inspired Adventure: An activity or experience providing an exhilarating journey into the world of natural beauty.
- *Writing* Inspired Adventure: An activity or experience providing an expressive journey into the world of intuitive journaling and storytelling.
- *Heart* Inspired Adventure: An activity or experience providing a compassionate journey into the world of kindness, love, and friendship.
- *Artfully* Inspired Adventure: An activity or experience providing a creative journey into the world of color, design, and self-expression.
- *Mystical* Inspired Adventure: An activity or experience providing a magical journey into the world of spirituality spirit signs and intuition.
- *Education* Inspired Adventure: An activity or experience providing an informative journey into the world of learning, study, and practice.
- *Entertainment* Inspired Adventure: An activity or experience providing an immersive journey into the world of imagination, sound, and amusement.
- *Wellness* Inspired Adventure: An activity or experience providing a healthy journey into the world of self-care, vitality, and well-being.

- *Zen* Inspired Adventure: An activity or experience providing a mindful journey into the world of peace, healing, and spiritual awareness.
- *Travel* Inspired Adventure: An activity or experience providing an expansive journey into the world of new horizons and views.

Questions to ask yourself:
- What activities make your heart sing?
- What are your true desires of the heart for healing?
- What activities, experiences, or adventures will help you lift the heaviness of grief toward emotional freedom?
- What soulful self-care practices do you find to improve your emotional health and well-being?
- Are you allowing new adventures and experiences to come into your life?
- What Soulful Inspired Adventure are you giving yourself today?
- What Soulful Inspired Adventure brings renewed peace to your life?
- What Soulful Inspired Adventure brings an invigorating expansion of hope to your life?
- What Soulful Inspired Adventure will you experience to uplift your spirit, nurture your soul, and fill your heart with lightness and joy?
- Will your Soulful Inspired Adventure today be inspired by nature, art, music, wellness, cuisine, heart, writing, Zen, or other activities?
- Will this Soulful Inspired Adventure be a solo experience or shared with friends and family?
- What Soulful Inspired Adventure did you experience and enjoy today?

Soulful Notes

_____
_____
_____
_____
_____
_____
_____
_____
_____
_____
_____
_____

It is through our awareness and enjoyment of our surroundings, our environment, our relationships, our choices on how we use our time, and how we care for our body, mind, and soul that we experience transformative healing.

As I looked upon these adventures as a way to celebrate life in memory of my daughters, I found it soothed my soul, nurtured my body, and comforted my heart. I became stronger, more purposeful, and soulfully adventurous in the process.

I invite you to join me in practicing soulful, inspired living as you discover ways to invigorate your soul, expand your perspective, and uplift your body, mind, and spirit with a sense of wonder and adventure.

Allow yourself to be expansive, to widen your boundaries around you to be less restrictive as you become more expressive in voice, activity, and creativity. Notice the experiences and Soulful Inspired Adventures that are available to you everywhere you go. Let yourself open up, little by little to the lighthearted possibilities waiting for you. Release the weight of seriousness and limitations that are part of your grief process. Truly, let yourself feel lighter and allow the illuminated energy to flow through you, breaking up old patterns of unhappiness and regret. You have so much to live for and to be joyful about in many areas of your life. Throw aside the heavy weight of grief and call in the energies of love, joy, compassion, and freedom to your heart and soul's journey.

Nature Inspired Adventure

An activity or experience providing an exhilarating journey into the world of natural beauty.

Cloud Watching – Star Gazing – Flower Arranging – Bird Watching – Walking in Nature – Gardening – Catch a Rainbow – Watch Sunrise or Sunset – Animal Encounters – Beach Day – Resting in a Hammock – Mountain View – Basking in the Sunshine – Enjoying the Weather – Viewing the Moon – Garden Shopping – Boating – Walking the Dog – Playing in the Snow – By the Lake – Wildflower Fest – Hiking – Swimming – Kayaking

Nature provides vibrant inspiration for all the world to see. Nature has amazing healing properties, and it is especially helpful to focus our attention on that which brings about peace and uplifting joy. Sometimes, that means simply observing the natural beauty around us.

Where in nature do you find yourself to truly be mindful, to feel peace & joy, calm and contentment, healing and rejuvenation, awestruck and inspired, uplifted and renewed, enlightened and energized?

Nature can provide one-of-a-kind adventures where you may discover something you've never seen before, such as a flower, leaf, pattern in the sky, or creature that stays with you for a while, leaving imprints upon your soul. Tap into the peace and essence of nature during times of uncertainty, confusion, or restlessness, as well as during those moments that require healing, such as illness, loss, or difficult life circumstances. Allow the sights and sounds of nature to bring a sense of calmness and energy to your being, causing you to pause, breathe deeply, reflect, and allow a peaceful smile to form in your heart and on your lips.

I encourage you to be mindful of the mystical and magical healing that nature can provide to your heart and soul. Allow your spirit to breathe in the color, light, and energy of a particular flower that you may encounter in your daily life, in the garden, in your home, or when you are out in the world. The botanical beauty and essence of flowers can have a profound effect on your healing journey. Flowers can even provide a sign from or provide a special connection to your loved one in spirit. Let yourself have a moment of quiet listening to your intuition to discover if there is a message for you waiting to be revealed.

As in nature, let your light shine brilliantly and brightly in all you do and all that you are. Don't let life's disappointment and heartache dull your sparkle or light. Set your sights high, raise your vibration and its intensity to a higher level of being. Let your self-confidence and courage be elevated as you realize the depth and beauty of your soul. Let it shine.

At the Beach

Nature's beauty is all around us when we visit the beach. It's shimmery sunshine over the sea, blue skies, birds, and scattered treasures in the sand all inspire us to be mindfully aware of the exquisite sights and sounds going on in this natural environment.

The restorative and energetic boost it provides to our spirits is undeniable. The feeling of peace that occurs when walking on the beach, immersed in our own thoughts, fully embracing the moment, and perhaps allowing the tide to carry away our grief, pain, or concerns, is a profound experience.

Throughout my life, I've lived near the coast at least part of each year, and visiting beach towns throughout the world has been a passion in reclaiming joy and restoring balance to my body and spirit in all the chapters, challenges, and changes that have transpired.

Sea and Sand

Ah, the beach, its salty air, sugar sand beneath my feet, in the sun and sea is where I like to be. A kite surfer breaks the silence with a flip and a splash. I breathe in deep and let it go with an audible sigh. The sea breeze dries my tears while the whitecaps drift by in the aqua surf, taking with it my sadness, leaving me to smile in the wonder of this beautiful day.

At the beach in Key West, I received this message from Crystal and a bird named Magic.

I am here with you at the beach, sending my love and the seagull that is staying with you. I love you, Mom. You are playing in my stomping grounds, and I want to share it with you. We are here with you as you soak in the healing rays of this beautiful beach day. Let the energy of nature sustain you. Let the warmth of the sun upon your chest open your heart and allow the healing rays to nurture you. May you be filled with radiant peace and joy. May God's grace shine upon you. Let the glistening ocean stimulate the creativity in your soul as you seek to express what's in your heart.

Red Cardinal Song

As I enjoyed my morning coffee on the deck one day at sunrise in Crystal Beach, a beautiful red cardinal stopped by to visit me for a while. Bursting out in a beautiful song. Its beauty, power, and strength were apparent in tone and stance, along with a healing message of peace and calmness, reminding me that we are not alone on this journey. Our loved ones, angels, and guides in spirit are living alongside us, offering love, encouragement, and hope every step of the way. Taking some time to sit in the stillness of life is crucial to nurturing our being, allowing restorative healing to take place in our hearts and souls.

Soulful Suggestion: Nature Exercise

Set your intention to be present at this time to reflect and connect with your soul. Allow yourself to become flexible as you let your guard down and breathe in this opportunity in nature to let go, to choose to live a life free from the heaviness and constraints of pain, suffering, and loss.

- *Imagine you are at the beach where each wave coming to shore washes over you, and one by one, layer by layer, the pain of your grief and trauma is lifted and carried away.*
- *Imagine you are climbing to a mountain top, and step by step, boulder by boulder, clinging and clawing along the dusty mountainside, only to feel reborn when you reach the top, taking in the expansive view while breathing in the fresh mountain air.*
- *Imagine you are sitting in your favorite tree. As you relax into the space, feeling safe and secure, let yourself take in the strength and resilience of this beautiful living energy. Notice the delicate leaves and sweetness of the blossoms, if there are any, and breathe in the natural beauty. Notice the tree trunk. Is it smooth with few knots, or is it weathered and rough? Either way is perfect because it is shaped by nature, and in generosity of spirit, accept it without judgment or criticism if you can. Accept yourself, too, with the beauty of your soul and all the lessons learned.*

As you go there in person today or in your mind's eye, imagine yourself to be present with the nature that surrounds you as you breathe in that which will add positivity to your well-being and breathe out, releasing that which no longer serves you at this time or is holding you back from living, fully. As you do, let your negative self-talk, hurtful experiences, and loss or grief of any kind wash away and be transmuted into healing energy for the planet. Ask the spirit world to assist in *providing an infusion of fresh, uplifted energy filled with light and joy into your being and life.*

Mindful Nature Meditation

In the outdoors, let your eyes gaze upon the view. Notice the cloud formations, the color of the sky, the varieties of nearby trees, or botanical beauty before you.

Take a deep breath and breathe in the fresh air. Is it salty or dry? Is it sweetly fragrant like orange blossoms or night-blooming jasmine, or is it scented like sage or pine? Depending on the season, the foliage may be vivid and green, blooming brightly, or autumn gold. As you continue to slowly breathe in and out, notice the energy from the sun radiating out to you. Feel the warmth upon your skin and draw in that powerful energy that only nature can provide. As you continue to breathe slowly, let go of the tension, discomfort, and grief that weigh on you and let them drift away among the landscape to be transmuted into healing light. Allow the energy of the sun to fill you with restorative healing and light, leaving you feeling renewed.

Questions to ask yourself:

- Have you meditated today?
- Have you tuned into your soul today?
- Have you allowed yourself time to sit in the stillness of peace today?
- What are your soul's desires today?
- What is your soul asking you to change about your life today?
- Did you send love and light to your soul today?
- Did you set an intention to experience uplifted living every day of the week?
- Do you long to discover what nourishes you to reclaim peace and joy in your life?

Soulful Notes

_____
_____
_____
_____
_____
_____
_____
_____
_____
_____
_____
_____

Take a moment each day to reflect on these questions and observe the effects and benefits you receive in connecting with your soul in new ways.

Heart Inspired Adventure

It is an activity or experience providing a compassionate journey into the world of kindness, love, and friendship.

Loving Gesture – Gift of Food or Flowers – Act of Generosity – Thoughtful Card – Self-love – Friendships – Lunch Date – Family Time – Moments of Connection – Romance – Emotional Support – Kindness – Compassion – Assistance – Invitations – Social Events – Heart Inspired Art – Kindness Rocks – Celebrations – Holidays

Your soul asks you to take special care of your heart, the loving center within your being. It has been hurt and regenerated many times in life, and it is the place where you feel the love that resides within you. The love that lets you know you are safe. The love that protects and

trusts. The love that carries worthiness that you are a beautiful soul with much to give to this world. Be confident. You can live from your heart. Let your soul feel free to shine in full expression. May you grow in the love and light that surrounds you to live a heart-centered life.

Be kind and patient with yourself. You are doing the best you can, and it's enough.

Sometimes, we are the hardest on ourselves, and yet it is up to us to manage our emotions, attitude, and state of mind. Give yourself a break.

Take a moment today to consider ways you can be kind to yourself. Whatever feels like self-care to you, do that, and do it often. When you are feeling generous, extend your kindness to the world around you.

May love radiate from your heart and soul to uplift your life in abundant ways.

We may never know what someone is going through, whether it is grief, sadness, depression, anxiety, pain, illness, or any other difficult or challenging situation, but being kind will impact lives in multiple ways you may not realize. Kindness has a way of smoothing the sharp edges of a broken heart, comforting and enlivening it.

A Lovely Gesture

Healing crystals are a wonderful tool that can provide many benefits depending on the stone. One day, as I was scrolling social media, I noticed a lovely post offering a crystal gemstone I had never seen before. It was an aqua aura quartz standing point, and it was gorgeous. The properties of it were just perfect at being known for stress relief, enhancing communication, psychic protection, and solace for the soul. A strong feeling came over me, and I felt it would be beneficial to my intuitive work, and I had to purchase it. Knowing it was the third anniversary of my daughter Crystal's celebration of life, I could feel her prompting me to do so in memory of her.

Its beautiful iridized aquamarine color was reminiscent of the shades of the ocean in the Florida Keys and Caribbean, where we shared our lives. When the order arrived in the mail, there was a special surprise tucked inside. It was a double heart quartz crystal, kindly added as a special gift. I immediately took this as a sign that both my daughters were united in love and guiding my journey in this life, and I appreciated Lisa's generosity and kindness. I still treasure these crystals and continue to use the aqua aura quartz to calm the emotions of grief and to quickly access the higher realms of communication of the spirit world in my mediumship work.

A Prayerful Gift

On a visit back to our former home of Crested Butte, Colorado, my husband and I attended a songwriter's fest that we have enjoyed in the past in this little village. As the concert was about to begin, I noticed the seat next to me was still empty. Suddenly, I felt the desire to go out into the hotel lobby and look around. There, I found someone who was without a seat and immediately offered him the one next to mine. It all happened so quickly, but I soon realized that this man was a priest and that he was a great supporter of musicians, especially those in recovery. It was a wonderful experience to share this concert with him, and I felt comforted in my grief in the process. Afterward, we stayed in touch, and one day, a beautiful, hand-crafted rosary arrived in the mail as a very kind gesture from this generous soul. It wasn't too long before another one arrived for my husband to treasure.

Cuisine Inspired Adventure

It is an activity or experience providing a delicious journey into the world of culinary art and libations.

QUESTION: Are you taking care of your physical health with nutritious foods and activity?

Baking – Dining Out – Picnic – Share Cooking – Try a New Restaurant – Family Recipes – Cooking Class – Creating Recipes – BBQ – Lunch or Dinner Date – Farmer's Market – Party Planning – Family Meals – Holidays – Coffee or Tea Time – Delicious Beverage – Healthy Food – Organic Produce – Vegetable or Herb Garden – Organize Kitchen

Culinary art and libations conjure up many facets of life experience and memories from early childhood to adulthood. Whether you enjoy shopping the markets and specialty stores for fresh ingredients to create meals at home or prefer dining in a variety of restaurants in your town or city, the food we consume packs more than a nutritional benefit. It feeds the soul in ways that are impossible to measure. I invite you to reflect on your memories related to the enjoyment of food. Do they include stories of loved ones no longer with you? Within every chapter of my life, there are fond cooking-related memories with loved ones now in spirit.

My grandparents on both sides lived close by and often a fresh treat was delivered for our family to enjoy. We also benefited from the lovingly prepared food from Annie, a wonderful woman who arrived in our bustling home when I was a young child and tenderly cared for our family for over three decades.

Some of my best food memories relate to my daughter, Crystal. Her passion for culinary arts was something that began in her childhood at home and in our natural food catering business. In her adult life, she thrived in commercial kitchens and we enjoyed sharing recipes, restaurant recommendations, and trying out new places together. Often when I am cooking for a family gathering, I can feel her presence with me so strongly, it brings tears and I can hear her reassuring me with a smile in her voice that all is well. She just wanted to share this experience with me again.

At this time, it is your Moment of Cuisine Inspired Adventure, and I ask you, in what ways could you provide nourishment and increased vitality to your body, mind, and soul? May you be nourished, nurtured, and soulfully satisfied by your cuisine inspired adventures.

Mystical Inspired Adventure

It is an activity or adventure providing a magical journey into the world of spirituality, spirit signs and intuition.

Card Reading – Mediumship Reading – Intuition – Spirit Signs – Spiritual Development Class – Read a Spiritual Book – Listening to Your Soul – Connecting with Spirit – Dreams and Visitations – Spirit Gifts – Crystals and Gemstones – Gemstone Jewelry – Magical Moments – Automatic Writing – Spirit Letters

Starlight Spirit Letter

I awoke one morning to a message from someone we had met a few months prior while we were staying in our RV on a visit to my stepson and his family. It was one of those magical meetings that spirit had arranged to provide an opportunity for her beautiful young granddaughter in spirit to send love and messages of support to her grandma through a chance meeting with us.

On the day we first met, we were standing in front of our campsite, and this lovely woman walked by with her dog. We greeted her and struck up a conversation, and something ignited the connection between us because immediately, within minutes of meeting each other, we joined her in walking her dog down the street.

It wasn't long before she expressed her traumatic loss that occurred less than a year prior. As I compassionately listened to her, I mentioned that I had experienced child loss, although I didn't mention that I was a medium. As we parted, I could, though, feel her granddaughter with us, and I began to hear a message especially meant for her grandma and her parents coming through.

When I returned to our RV, I sat inside and wrote down each loving word in a Starlight Inspired Letter and knew I had to find a way to deliver it to this grieving grandma who longed for it. I decided to take a walk through the RV park to see if I would see her again to let her know I was a medium and that I'd be happy to meet with her.

Within a few moments, she rode by on her golf cart, and we recognized each other with a hello, but she didn't stop. Encouraged but still looking for a moment to connect more deeply with her, I asked the spirit world to help, and I began walking back toward our campsite. By the time I arrived, she had driven by looking for me, and we were able to exchange contact info and make a plan to meet the following day.

In our session, I was able to share comforting and compassionate messages from her granddaughter with her that she was able to share with her family. It was a beautiful and heartfelt experience, and subsequently, I have shared several Soulful Starlight Sessions with her.

Later, she wrote to me that she had become aware of the signs she is given on a regular basis from her sweet granddaughter with a comment for me stating that I made it possible for her to feel calmer and at peace in the comfort of understanding her granddaughter was safe, happy and still with her. Her beautiful spirit shines bright with love for her family.

A Mystical Friendship

Within a few weeks after Crystal's passing, a dear friend in our little town of Crested Butte, where we lived, generously offered to give me an ortho-bionomy session, which is known to ease stress and increase healing from within through the nervous system. It was a gentle and reassuring experience of being nurtured and cared for in the fragile state I was in. It also paved the way for my being able to assist her at a later date after the loss of her beloved brother.

Through our mediumship session, she was able to receive evidence and encouragement from him of his love for her always. This allowed her to feel more at peace with his loss, knowing he was still with her and guiding her path. In subsequent sessions, she received further reassurance of his continued presence, easing her grief and helping her to remain open to the signs of spirit. When my beautiful friend left this world, she reached out almost immediately to let me know of her joyous arrival in the afterlife. I continue to feel her love, presence, and encouragement in my life, and I have many wonderful memories to recall of feeling cherished by her.

On Butterfly Wings

It's always a mystical magical experience to receive a visit from a beautiful butterfly. Yellow is a color that reminds me that my daughter, Crystal, in spirit, is near, and she presents signs in many ways that bring uplifting comfort and confirmation of her continued presence in my life.

One early morning near the sixth anniversary of her passing, as I walked around our Santa Fe backyard, I became aware of a gorgeous, large, and yellow butterfly sitting on the edge of our water fountain. I had observed this butterfly in our backyard since we arrived home a few days prior and was grateful for its presence. After taking a dip in the water, this beautiful tiger swallowtail enjoyed meandering through our flower garden as I stood watching from a few feet away for about ten minutes.

A home technician happened to be outside with me at the time, and we were both excited to witness the gentle and patient presence of this butterfly. My intuition kept prompting me to say something out loud that I debated on sharing with a stranger. As more time passed while the butterfly seemed in no hurry to leave, I couldn't contain my feelings about this being a sign from the afterlife any longer. My daughter passed away a few years ago, and she often sends a sign to me through the visit of a yellow butterfly, I softly say out loud. His response was immediate and heartfelt as he began to express that his best friend had passed not too long ago and recently sent him a white butterfly to confirm that he was still with him. We both discussed that it's not that they become the butterfly, only that they send them to delight, amaze, and confirm their presence from spirit.

We both felt the importance of receiving signs from heaven and were so grateful for the gift of this one when, suddenly, the butterfly lifted off the ground and landed on my hip. Stunned, I froze and quietly smiled as we both watched with pure amazement as this butterfly crawled up to sit on the belt around my waist. After a long minute or two, she began a slow climb up to my shoulder, where she stayed for another five minutes before flying off and over the adobe wall.

Thankfully, someone was there who was equally touched by this mystical and magical moment to share in the joy and capture it in a series of photos. It was a comforting and reassuring sign, combined with a butterfly just like this one that swirled around my head a few times while I sat in the garden just a few days before this experience.

It truly was an exquisite reminder that signs from our loved ones in spirit can uplift, comfort, and encourage us always.

Writing Inspired Adventure

It is an activity or experience providing an expressive journey into the world of intuitive journaling and storytelling.

Soulful Journaling – Creative Writing – Blog – Pour Your Heart Out – Book Club – Writing Group – Writing Workshop – Book Writing – Book Events – New Journal – Automatic Writing

Let your soul express what it needs to heal. Let it all out, let it pour into the page as it comes, don't censor it, don't block its full expression. Let your emotion direct its tone and depth. Let soulful journaling be a way out of sadness as you release what's waiting to be expressed. Tell your journal about your experiences, how you feel, and what you would like to achieve in your process of transforming grief into one that lives more comfortably within you, as a softer, more peaceful grief partner.

In my life, each time I was able to express in words, healing occurred. Expressing my emotions verbally was something I had to learn to do once I was in a loving and supportive relationship, but writing in a journal came easy and brought me back to hope from the depths of despair for many years. In times of crisis, creativity or calm, writing each day and listening to my intuition as I did, has played a crucial role in my life in moving forward, in my spirituality, and in my grief journey. The guidance I received from the spirit world included many modalities, practices, techniques, and adventures to assist in moving forward with intention, purpose, and passion, along with a gratefulness for the uplifting comfort I received in the process.

By allowing these emotions and feelings of loss, sadness, and regret to be expressed and released from our body, heart, and soul, little by little, our spirit is uplifted, our grief is lightened, and our heart gently opens to the love available to us.

I encourage you to pick up your journal again and see what happens as you write from your emotions, your heart, and your beautiful soul. Listen to your intuition and be expressive in your descriptions. Also, try asking the spirit world or one of your spirit guides to assist you at this time in your life and write down what is whispered to you in your intuition.

Soulful Suggestion: Soulful Intuitive Writing

Write a letter to your current self, describing how you are feeling, any blessings in your life, and the love and gratitude you still have for your loved one, no matter how long it's been since their passing. Allow yourself to step outside of the pain this person's death caused you and allow your heart to feel only love for this individual as you write about it.

Write a letter to your loved one in spirit expressing how you feel. If you could talk to someone in heaven, who would it be? What relationship would you most like to experience healing with in heaven? Would you be offering an apology or hoping to receive one so that forgiveness can occur? If you could receive a message, a sign, or a letter from someone in heaven, who would you choose?

Write one memory or story about your loved one that brings a smile.

Write something that contributed to your healing from grief in uplifting ways.

Write about an experience where life intersected with a magical adventure.

Write about the emotions you are experiencing in your grief and loss journey.

Education Inspired Adventure

It is an activity or experience providing an informational journey into the world of learning, study, and practice.

Workshop – Class – Seminar – Expo – Conference – Teacher Training – Certification – Online School – Course – Continuing Education – Library – Study Group – Lecture

Developing a new skill, studying a new craft, or practicing something you enjoy is a valuable pursuit in discovering and expressing your passion and opening new doors to expanded thinking. Whether you engage in a workshop, class, or training to improve your life and or the lives of others in service, the activity and experience of participating in it will benefit you in immense ways.

Stepping into a new environment of learning can provide unlimited opportunities to grow as you seek healing to integrate your loss in healthy ways. In my grief journey with Lavender, I learned to meditate, practice Reiki, and became a passionate student of the metaphysical arts, which widened my perspective and created a healthy platform in which to move forward while still holding her memory close. I pursued entrepreneurial business in natural food, flowers, art, interior design, massage therapy, and fused glass and beaded jewelry, as well as explored my early mediumship abilities.

Following Crystal's passing, I immersed myself in the study and practice of intuitive writing and mindfulness, becoming a Reiki master, receiving certifications in spiritual life coaching, happiness coaching, therapeutic art coaching, and advanced mediumship, and I learned to write and publish this book in the process.

In the pursuit of each new skill, my mind was engaged in positive ways, and yet when my emotions called for it, I let them lead the way. I had new tools and inspiration to assist in my grieving process that allowed greater understanding and knowledge of ways to foster self-nurturing that was beneficial to my entire being. It also helped immensely to realize that I could inspire others to discover a path to release the trauma and infuse their life with hope, compassion, and creativity through these many avenues.

Your journey will look different than mine, but I encourage you to explore areas of interest to add an infusion of new ideas to your life in colorful and creative ways.

At this time, it is your Moment of Education Inspired Adventure, and I ask you, in what ways could you expand your life experience to include inspiration, insights, and a desire to learn something new?

Entertainment Inspired Adventure

It is an activity or adventure providing an immersive journey into the world of imagination, sound, and amusement.

Watch a Movie – Visit Local Library – Browse a Bookstore – Comedy Show – Stream a Favorite Program – Go to the Theatre – Dinner and a Play – Concert – Performance – Live Music – Jam Session – Play an Instrument – Read New Book – Travel – Expand your View

Sound therapy and music fill the soul with joy, uplift the spirit, and connect you to a melodic wave of creativity and positive energy or peace and calm. Whether you are enjoying it by yourself or in the company of other music lovers, the experience of hearing music may cause you to intently listen to the lyrics and instruments, sway from side to side, dance wildly, or be transported to a previous time in memory of a loved one.

Music enhances all aspects of our lives as it plays in the background of daily living. It awakens and motivates us on road trips, commutes to work, and on errands. It enhances the experiences of meal preparation and dining itself. Music adds a beautiful backdrop to special occasions, parties, and social events. Discovering your preference for a style of music, favorite performer, or band is an entertaining process and a personal experience that is often heightened by sharing it with family and friends. Whatever your style of music and whether you prefer playing music or just listening to others who are passionate about their craft, I suggest you let it be a soulful, inspired adventure, bringing much happiness and healing to all the days of your life.

Documentaries, movies, streaming shows, books, and all forms of entertainment have value in inspiring, informing, entertaining, or uplifting you when you immerse yourself in the experience. Watching a comedy show, movie, or comedian offers something extra in that it encourages you to let go of your emotions and experience laughter. Just letting yourself smile, laugh a little, or laugh out loud is beneficial to your overall health and state of mind.

May you discover the perfect entertainment that brings enjoyment to your body, mind, and soul.

Artfully Inspired Adventure

It is an activity or experience providing a creative journey into the world of color, design, and self-expression.

Intuitive Painting – Collage – Drawing – Mandala – Vision Board – Art Date – Kindness Rocks – Jewelry Design – Photography – Art Class – Sewing – Interior Design – Art Destinations – Crafting – Color Play – Pottery or Clay Work – Outdoor Art – Art Therapy – Garden Design

Art Adventures:
- Abstract collage using gorgeous paper.
- Handmade ornaments for holiday trees.
- Mosaic designs using gems and broken plates.
- Baking holiday gifts for yourself and loved ones.
- Natural mandala with stones, leaves, and crystals.
- Drawing your animal spirit guides: horses, deer, birds, rabbits, etc.

Soulful Inspired Adventures

- Stamping, stencils, and printmaking.
- Painting colorful wooden hearts or other shapes.
- Watercolor rainbows with shimmering glitter.
- Letter writing with pressed wax stamps.
- Artful journaling from your soul in a beautiful book.
- Vision board with clipped words and phrases.
- Painting kindness rocks.
- Graphic art and design.
- Designing a garden.
- Write words and or music for a song.
- Creating a photo book.
- Art show, museum, or art gallery.
- Painting a mural or walls in your home.
- Take a class online or in person.

Wake up and observe your state of mind.

Choose happiness and immerse yourself in thoughts and experiences that provide a colorful lift and a lightness to your soul. Allow yourself time, space, and permission to experience creativity in all the ways that uplift and add joy to your life.

Adding fresh new colors to your world can bring a smile each time you encounter them. Consider how you may add color to your surroundings inside and outdoors.

- Paint your front door inside and out in a shade of your favorite color.
- Place your favorite botanical bouquet or plant on your dining table.
- Add a luscious assortment of fresh fruit to your favorite bowl in the kitchen.
- Enhance your dining experience with vivid and fun placemats or tablecloths.
- Embellish your bed with bright, happy pillowcases or shams.
- Hang a pretty garland in your windows to enliven the view.

- String twinkling lights in a doorway, around a mirror, or a mantle.
- Decorate the garden with colorful banners, prayer flags, statues, and flowers.
- Start a kindness rock garden for yourself or your neighbors.
- Hang photos of nature that you find uplifting and beautiful.

After the hurricane repairs were completed at our home in Crystal Beach by a skilled and caring friend, it was time to choose paint colors. As I stood in front of the display with hundreds of samples in front of me, my eyes couldn't believe the name I observed on one of the paint chips. It was a name of a color unlike any I'd ever observed in all the years of decorating homes. "Love, Crystal" was a pretty color of gray, similar to the shade our walls had been painted before the hurricane. It was a wonderful reminder of her continued presence in our home and life and I appreciated receiving it.

A few years ago, I had the pleasure of visiting with my dad's cousin at a family gathering. She was a woman I hadn't seen since childhood. It only took a few moments after our excited greetings to stand before each other as two mothers who have experienced the loss of an adult child. As we stared into each other's eyes, there was a deep understanding and great compassion for the grief each of us has experienced. I listened to her describe her son's passing, and I could see him there with us in my mind. He was looking well and smiling.

Immediately, I found myself consoling her as she struggled with the fact that her son had passed away suddenly, alone and away from her. As difficult as that is, I said, "I believe that in some way I wasn't meant to be there at the time of my daughter Crystal's transition to spirit, and the pain and regret about it remained for some time." I reminded this grieving mom that our children are still with us and wish for us to discover ways to enjoy life again. And with that, we agreed with both, knowing it is an ongoing journey to reclaiming joy after experiencing a traumatic loss.

When she asked if I've always been an artist, I expressed to her that art and creativity hold an important role in my grief journey. There is so much beauty in our natural world to experience and express through the creative arts, photography, and writing, and each has provided an abundance of uplifting and inspiring experiences in my life.

Each day, we are given the opportunity to express how we are feeling in words, pictures, paintings, songs, and various other activities, passions, and pursuits. Self-expression frees your soul to breathe. It infuses your life with color, pattern, and design, or song and music, in your own artistic expression or appreciating that of another. When we express what's in our hearts, it gives our life a sense of meaning and purpose.

Self-expression comes in many forms, and it may be colorful and bright or somber and gray. It doesn't matter as long as it comforts and soothes your heart.

At this time, it is your Moment of Artfully Inspired Adventure, and I ask you, in what ways could you let your imagination go?

Allow yourself to be expansive, to widen your boundaries around you to be less restrictive as you become more expressive in voice, activity, and creativity.

What creative adventures will you explore to discover more healing, hope, and happiness in your life? What self-expression is calling out to be expressed through you?

I invite you to experience an artfully inspired adventure that uplifts and nurtures your body, mind, and soul as you pause in the process of soulful adventuring.

Introducing the children in your life to a playful project can have a profound effect on your emotional well-being. Sharing a love of creative expression and creating artful gifts with our young granddaughter has been immensely enjoyable, and many days have been filled with painting rocks and shells, smearing paint on canvas, layering paper with glue, stamping with colorful inks, drawing with watercolors, all expanding her awareness for learning about the colorful world of art and creativity, self-expression and about generosity and kindness. In our home, we play music, sing and dance, and read aloud, encouraging freedom to be expressive with movement and words. Let song and music fill the background or the foreground of your life.

Soulful Suggestions

Discovering a kindness rock is a gift that holds within it a gesture of kindness, healing, and love. If you find a painted rock, you are invited to keep it, leave it, or share it with someone else as a gesture of kindness. Posting it on social media and tagging the artist lets them know it has been found and enjoyed. The variety of artists of all ages creating colorful little treasures to give away is astounding in style and creativity. Let yourself be inspired to join in the kindness movement in any way you choose.

If you find one of mine with #soulfulkindnessrocks please share a pic on social media and tag me @theartofsoulfulinspiredliving

A Mermaid Adventure

One day, while my husband and I were out exploring a nearby coastal town of Gulfport, we discovered a little shop that had a beautiful outdoor mermaid statue. Upon seeing it, I thought of my daughter, Crystal, and just knew we had to buy it for our front yard. Immediately, I began creating a mermaid garden for our young granddaughter to enjoy, with this mermaid statue as the focal point. I gave her the name Loralie after Crystal and later added a bunny statue I named Lavender. Our granddaughter has treasured this garden and was so grateful it survived the feet of water that flooded our yard during the two hurricanes of 2024. We both enjoy adding our painted rocks and shells among the stones and colored gems and decorating the garden for the holidays.

Whether your creative expression is solo or in the company of others, you will be uplifted by the experience and take that positivity with you out into the world. We could all use a little more playful enthusiasm and joy, infusing our lives with energy. If you are following the stirrings of your heart, forge ahead with abundant freedom to express and allow yourself to take in the essence of an artful event because it just feels good.

Creating art for yourself or others is a healing practice, an art therapy, and I am certain it soothes your soul, engages your spirit, and enlivens your heart in whatever form it takes.

May today be the beginning of a new chapter of creative and expressive healing in your life.

EXERCISE: Draw six hearts on a page, one each for your spiritual body, physical body, emotional body, relationships, passions, and outreach. As you go into meditation, ask one of your spirit guides to provide a word or message on all six of these hearts to expand your awareness and guide you forward in love and light.

Soulful Notes

Another creative suggestion is to design a vision board, an art journal, or art collage cards that you enjoy making and will also enjoy looking at with intention for the desires of your heart.

PROJECT: Power of Intention Art Collage

- Create something inspiring and set it up where you see it each day.
- Start with a magnetic board, cork board, large sheet of sturdy paper, or playing cards.
- Cut out words or phrases or write out desired words, desires, affirmations, and quotes.
- Use magazine clippings or craft materials to compile words that inspire you.
- Add pictures of your goals and desires on your healing journey.
- It can be simple or very decorated, just so you enjoy creating it.

Colorize Your Life

Magnificent and magical
luscious and lighthearted
energetic and energized
dazzling and dramatic
soft and serene
infuse your world with beauty, color, and light

Wellness Inspired Adventure

It is an activity or adventure providing a healthy journey into the world of self-care, vitality and well-being.

Working Out – Walking – Hiking – Biking – Swimming – Dancing – Bubble Baths – Raise Your Vibration – Chakra Balancing – Running Your Energy – Extra Rest – Grief Release – Body Care –

Chiropractic – Healthy Eating – Nutrition – Sleep – Preventive Healthcare – Travel – Joining Groups – Spiritual Practice – Financial Balance – Personal Habits – Reiki Energy

Welcome to a moment of Soulful Inspired Wellness. It is your moment to nurture your well-being. What areas of wellness could provide nourishment and increased balance to your state of being and your physical, mental, and emotional health?

You are on a new path to well-being. It's important that you realize the value of taking care of yourself. Health is everything. Vitality is not a given. One must discover ways to stay active physically, mentally, and creatively as they age. Emotional health is something that can also be improved in many ways. Find your groove, your routine, and your program of ways to create soulful awareness and wellness in your life every day.

Being aware of your thoughts, emotions, and energy level is crucial to determine the type of healing activity necessary for the day. If you are weary, then a healing meditation would be beneficial. If you are anxious, then a nature walk can be helpful. If you are feeling sad, then a lunch or coffee date with a nurturing friend would be helpful. If you are feeling overwhelmed, then a session with a compassionate therapist or coach can be immensely beneficial. If you're feeling unmotivated, creating something colorful, musical, or delicious can be helpful. If you feel unloved, then offer generosity to another person. If your body feels tense, then a therapeutic massage is in order. If your emotions are feeling flat, then reading or listening to an uplifting book or speaker is invaluable. There are so many ways to take care of your body, mind, and soul, and I invite you to choose wisely based on your intuition and current situation.

May today be the beginning of improved wellness in your body, mind, and spirit.

Reiki Energy

My Reiki journey began many years ago, and it has sustained my life through devastating changes and overwhelming challenges, assisting me to balance my energy, provide healing to my heart, strengthen my weary spirit, and fuel my light-filled mission to not only survive trauma but also to light the path for others along the way. Holding onto these heavy emotions is restrictive and limits our ability to listen to our intuition and to receive clarity, as well as physical comfort within our own bodies.

Questions to ask yourself:

- What emotions are you holding onto that you would like to release?
- What sensations are you experiencing in your body at this moment: tightness in your chest, fear of the present or future, uneasiness or discontent, anger, hurt, disappointment in others or world events?

Soulful Notes

Zen Inspired Adventure

It is an activity or adventure providing a mindful journey into peace, healing and spiritual awareness.

Meditation – Being Present – Self Reflection – Relaxing Atmosphere – Tea Time – Exercise – Walking Meditation – Gratitude – Unwinding – Declutter – Patience – Persistence – Mindful Breathing – Yoga – Pilates – Mindful Art – Observe Thoughts without Judgment – Relaxation – Massage – Energy Work

There are many ways to achieve a sense of Zen in your life that is beneficial to your health and feels wonderfully uplifting.

Being outdoors, walking or sitting in nature, listening to the sounds of birds or the peace and quiet, provides a space to breathe, to reflect, and to listen to the spirit world and your own soul. You may receive healing or inspiration for a situation you are experiencing or a creative project you may be working on.

It is through mindful meditation of being in the moment that you may discover a delightful sight in nature that catches your eye and uplifts your entire being.

Many find support and encouragement in practicing yoga, pilates, or other mindful exercises, as well as meditation and self-reflection. Receiving energy work, massage therapy, or Reiki can also create a feeling of Zen in your body that is nurturing and healing.

This is your Moment of Zen Inspired Adventure; how will you use it to uplift and nurture your body and soul?

I wish for you mystical, magical, mindful moments to uplift, nurture, and restore your body, mind, and spirit for the days, weeks, and years ahead.

Travel Inspired Adventure

It is an activity or experience providing an expansive journey into the world of new horizons and views.

Cruise – Camping – Road Trips – Airplane – Resorts – Vacation – Staycation – Boat – Ferry – Taxi – Driving Service – Shuttle – Bus – Train – RV – Explore

Travel adventures take you on a journey that evokes a mindfulness of being present in the moment as you are living it. Every aspect of the environment, weather, sights, scenes, and sounds all provide a colorful escape for your body, mind, and spirit. Experiencing a new culture or the history of a new city or town expands your perspective and infuses your world with a greater awareness of life beyond your own. Travel can add a refreshing burst of enjoyment to your present reality. Nature in a new locale can provide unlimited views that uplift and regional cuisine can stimulate your senses to new tastes and flavors.

Depending on your preference, whether you stay in hotels or vacation rentals, visit the mountains, the desert, or the sea. There are opportunities for comfort and well-being in whichever way you choose.

As you travel, you may receive signs that your loved one is along for the ride with you. I feel Crystal's presence nearly every time I am going somewhere by car, especially on road trips or someplace that is meaningful to her. When we visited Hope Town, Bahamas, a few years ago, I could feel her presence with us as we traveled to her familiar places. Afterward, she recounted to me how much she enjoyed our trip and the comical parts that made her smile as she watched us from her vantage point.

On that trip, I also received a spirit message from a man who was a close family friend who passed a short time before our arrival on the island. He explained many things to me about his life and thanked me for meeting with his wife on that trip, whom I had not met prior to his passing. He let me know he was with my dad and step-mom and their dog, Salty, and that they enjoy fishing together in the afterlife, clearly as much as they did in their life on earth.

Where will you experience Travel inspired Adventures in the coming year? Will it be by the mountains or the sea, the city or open landscape? How will you travel, by car or cruise ship, camper or caravan, airline or small charter plane? If travel to distant places isn't a possibility, will you explore new environments in your nearby city or town that provide opportunities to uplift and expand your horizons?

Happy Soulful Adventuring!

Twenty Five
Soulful Adventures Challenge

>>>>----

"When you are deep in a transformational process, set your intention to heal with soulful resilience and strength. Be intentional yet flexible, and soon, you will be moving forward feeling lighter through these difficult life emotions. Allow yourself to be centered in love, light, and passion for your life again."

—**Nancy Yuskaitis, *Soulful Starlights***

A self-care challenge offering a new opportunity to uplift, heal, and reclaim joy in your life while fostering resilience by discovering the simple act of mindfulness through soulful, inspired adventures.

Every day, we are given the opportunity to observe the experiences and activities that add value, comfort, or healing to our lives and to breathe in that upliftment with expanded awareness as it nurtures our well-being.

All that is required is for you to have the presence of mind to observe and enjoy the uplifting effects of experiencing something inspiring, colorful, delightful, delicious, beautiful, or encouraging at least once each day.

Anyone can do this challenge, and it is an ideal way to stay mindful of your soulful self-care and to offer a lightness to your grief as these simple yet powerful activities can provide comfort and relief from the heaviness of sorrow toward a more peaceful way to live with your grief.

These moments are filled with adventures and mindful awareness of the natural beauty and enjoyment that can be discovered in everyday experiences in our lives. Simply being aware and fully present to observe the cloud formations in the sky, a beautiful animal sighting, a delicious beverage or meal, an artful scene, a kind gesture, a new bloom in your garden, an uplifting passage in a book, or a spirit sign from the universe can provide immense healing and uplifted living.

Joining this challenge can assist in encouraging you to evolve in ways to heal anew in a gentle process of gradually uplifting your well-being in many areas of your life. It is a way to be more present in our relationships with family and friends, in using creativity and intuition to guide you through loss with new energy and focus.

To begin, each day:
- Check in with yourself.
- Nurture your well-being.
- Read something inspiring.
- Spend time in nature.
- Practice soulful self-care.
- Write in your journal or express your creativity.
- Sit in the stillness of meditation or prayer.
- Allow yourself to feel uplifted by enjoyable experiences.
- Experience at least one Soulful Inspired Adventure.

Soulful Suggestions for You: Simply choose an uplifting activity or intention to experience from my list, or you may observe something in your own life that fits as an inspired Adventure to create your personal healing challenge. Just remember to observe at least one enjoyable activity, adventure, or experience each day that infuses your life with contentment and gratitude.

Artful – Cuisine – Friendship – Heartfelt – Fitness – Laughter – Libation – Music – Nature – Mystical – Magical – Mindfulness – Spirituality – Creativity – Love – Dance – Self-care – Writing – Zen – Reading – A Workshop – Meditation – Class – Event – Concert – Coffee Date – High Tea – Picnic – Beach Walk – Sunset View – Play – Bodywork – Yoga – Outdoor Fitness – Gym – Spa Movie – Series – Comedy – Bike Ride – Kayak – Hike – Garden

Make a Promise to Yourself

I promise to allow mystical, magical, mindful moments and soulful-inspired adventures to reclaim, restore, and renew my passion and joy for living alongside my grief.

Each week, list six activities or experiences that you intend to experience or have experienced that will most certainly offer you a lightness of heart and a nurturing sense of renewed hope with the possibility of reclaimed joy. Consider all the types of adventures you may seek to experience in art, creativity, expressive writing, music, dance, yoga, fitness, cuisine, libations, energy healing, meditation, spirituality, friendship, nature, love, and travel.

To keep you inspired, you may wish to record or document your adventures in a calendar, notebook, journal, or meme to track and share your times of enjoyment. You can also use colorful stickers or markers to track the emotional benefit received in each activity. Notice how the activity or experience made you feel. Extremely uplifted or just moderately so. Remember that each day will build upon the one before, increasing your ability to notice, accept, and string together happy moments in your life.

Even when you feel too sad to participate in a soulful, inspired adventure, I encourage you to keep an open heart that is mindful of the unexpected experiences in everyday life that may uplift and delight you in mystical, magical, and mindful moments. These moments of uplift certainly count.

Questions to ask yourself:

- What Soulful Inspired Adventure did I experience today?
- Which Soulful Inspired Adventure did I feel created a bit of uplifting joy?
- Which Soulful Inspired Adventure brought about a feeling of peace?
- Did I enjoy a solo Soulful Inspired Adventure or one shared with others?
- Was it inspired by nature, cuisine, entertainment, creativity, self-care, etc.?
- Did you notice how each activity or experience made you feel?

Soulful Notes

_____
_____
_____
_____
_____
_____
_____
_____
_____
_____
_____
_____
_____

I invite you to join my transformational journey from traumatic loss to uplifted well-being, to be inspired to participate each day or when it feels right for you.

You are encouraged to share your Soulful Inspired Adventures with us and the community and to inspire others along their soulful, inspired journey. You can do so by using #soulfulinspiredadventureschallenge and or sharing in our Facebook group @hopeloveandtheafterlife. Be sure also to follow @The Art of Soulful Inspired Living to stay up to date with insight and inspiration.

NOW IS YOUR TIME TO:

- Live in the present.
- Bask in the Sunshine.
- Practice Self-Love.
- Embrace Love and Light.
- Be Yourself.
- Encourage Others.
- Express Creatively.
- Reclaim Joy.
- Listen to your Intuition.
- Seek Inner Peace.
- Learn Something New.
- Celebrate Life.
- Offer Kindness and Compassion.
- Experience Soulful Inspired Adventures.

Twenty Six
Soulful Messages

"Time is of the essence. Do not let another day go by without taking steps to allow moments of light-filled joy into your awareness."

—*Nancy Yuskaitis*

The following messages of love were sent to me by my daughters, angels, and spirit guides, and I share them as they are also meant for you. I hope the sentiments contained within, along with this book, bring comfort and confidence that you are not walking this healing journey alone. Your loved ones are walking it with you, offering peace, compassion, and a new understanding of life after life.

Soulful Starlights' Message to You

Stay centered, stay strong, soak in the beauty of nature, and allow yourself to be transformed in the process. Don't ever let your sparkle be dimmed by your disappointment in how others respond to your grief process. Not everyone is meant to feel the way you do, and that's okay. Let your light shine, anyway.

In this life, you may touch the hearts of those who never let on the significance of your presence in their life. Shine your light anyway.

Bask in the knowing that you can impact lives and uplift souls each day that you are alive. Live like you are fully alive. Live passionately, vividly, and be consciously aware of the beautiful souls who share this life with you, seen and unseen.

Everywhere you go, you have a team of angels, guides, and loved ones supporting, protecting, and encouraging you each step of the way. Being grateful for this universal presence is undoubtedly felt and multiplied within you.

Message for Parents after an Overdose

I am so sorry for your heartbreak and the loss of your beautiful child. Sometimes, the journey of addiction is short, and other times quite long, as it was for my daughter, but it still leaves you unable to breathe with the crushing sorrow you are left with after a sudden overdose. Let your loved one live in your heart and comfort you as you scream, cry, express, and grieve. It's true the pain never entirely leaves, but it can soften with time and grief work. Be kind, gentle, and patient with yourself from moment to moment, each step of the way. As the waves of grief wash over you, let them come, then let them go, leaving you more resilient and filled with purpose to care for yourself and your family. Peace be with you.

Message for Those Providing Grief Support

Dear Beautiful Soul, may you recognize the profound impact you can have on others through your conscious, loving light. Your ability and awareness of the spirit world are limitless. Your focus and desire to access thoughts, impressions, and messages are enhanced by your open, gracious heart and generosity. Your loving spiritual soul is graced and guided in protective healing, insightful energy, and light.

You each hold within you the intensity to be a light force, a lighthouse, a beacon of hope in a world where darkness is always looming. You all possess great strength and well-being, resilience and restoration, hope and harmony, and love beyond words. You are supported and loved by the spirit world in every area of your life. Whether you are dealing with a health issue, relationship disharmony, a transition in lifestyle, or a broken heart due to loss, you need to look no further than your own heart and soul. Call upon the angels and guides to work with you in your desire to be of service, but do not forget to take care and listen to your soul. You are most valuable to others when you are feeling healthy, vibrant, and whole.

Message for Parents of a Child in Heaven

You are my world. You are pure love. You are never alone. My immense love is with you with every step you take. I send blessings of grace, wonder, and hope to your heart. Thank you for your unconditional love, encouragement, and guidance, always. I love you!

Angel Message to Parents after a Child's Overdose

We are aware of the painful emotions you are experiencing, and we send you an abundance of comfort to ease your sorrow. This is a dreadful situation, yet we send you hope that you may realize your child's struggle is over and is reborn with strength and vitality unlike any they were able to experience on earth. It's important that you understand that this wasn't your fault and to please forgive yourself. Peace has been found, and now it is being sent to you with a wish that you take the beautiful essence of your child with you as you move forward in your life. Let yourself be comforted in the love that will always remain between you, always and forever.

Your child is reborn with vitality and a strength they were unable to master in this life. Eternal love and gratitude are being sent to you for all your positive intentions, assistance, and loyalty to their well-being and beautiful souls.

Throughout their addiction, so many emotions were experienced by each of you in times of rejoicing and renewal, in struggle and despair, and now it's important for you to know that you didn't fail your child by being unable to save them. This was their journey, and now they have found peace. Their desire now is for you to find the peace and healing necessary to live out your life experience. Take what you can of your child's essence deep into your soul and hold it with you as you grieve. Let yourself find peace within the love that will always remain between their beautiful soul and yours.

A Message from Your Soul

I am here. You are here. We are one.
Allow yourself to breathe in this oneness.
Allow yourself to soak up this moment of strength in being.
Your soul is resilient, it is hopeful, and it is free from such heaviness.
Breathe in this freedom, the freshness of being.
Know that even when you feel sadness or separation, your loved ones are comforting you on the wings of angels.

Message to Parents about Addiction

Lavender's loyal presence has comforted, consoled, and counseled me for many decades. She provided much insight and an abundance of compassion as my daughter, and in this message, she was trying to help me understand the struggles her sister, Crystal, faced for many years, knowing how painful it was for me to not be able to save her from suffering in her addiction.

There are some souls whose path on earth is a difficult one. They may be a soul who just can't seem to understand life at all. It is a mystery to them. There is not a clearly defined path for them to follow. Sometimes, they possess a great deal of common sense, yet their emotional quotient is very low.

Sometimes, they hold back from participating in their own life fully by thinking they need to rescue others. In a way, this gives them fulfillment, albeit a temporary sense of being needed. They spend their energy rescuing other lost souls who use them and then throw them away. Some require very little in the way of material things and stability. This would bother most people, but for some, having the responsibilities of it is too stressful.

At times, some people may need to be loved from a distance so that they may create their own life. We cannot do someone else's personal work for them. Their fear of being alone causes a disservice because no one can shield us from our lessons. This only distracts us from growing in ways that are right for us.

As much as the spirit world is asked to intervene, in many situations, free will determines their destiny. As similar as we are as human beings, we each individually have our life's purpose to work out. This may be painful as we watch our loved ones struggle with unhealthy choices and difficult consequences and are unable to impact the situation as we wish. It may even diminish our energy and dim our light, but we must try our best to remain open to experiencing joy as well as life's wonder and beauty. Take care of yourself and keep your own light strong and vibrant. After all, it is your life, too, and you don't want to miss a precious moment of life's pleasures and grace. Wishing you love, peaceful light, and happiness always.

Prayer for Love and Healing

May I be surrounded by the essence of love. May the vibration of love begin in me and rise in a pink spiral of love throughout my body, clearing pain and heartbreak or any emotional suffering remaining within my body. May any tension around my emotional body be released, allowing the fullness of love to be seen, felt, and heard. May this pink light comfort, restore, and rebalance the energy of emotion within my heart chakra. May my throat area be cleared to speak words of love, acceptance, and understanding to myself, my family, my friends, and beyond. I allow this light to open my sense of self-love and harmony as my spirit and soul connect with the universal power of love that transforms lives. I bask in the wonderment of love. I am loved and loving in all ways.

Affirmations for Healing

- I may have been through some rough times and devastating storms, but I am still standing strong and brave.
- I am replenished by the love and light that surrounds me.
- I allow my heart to be filled with love and my spirit to shine with joy.
- I live with an open heart, a full heart, and a compassionate heart, with boundaries and limits in place for self-protection, self-reflection, and soulful self-care.
- I live a life of healthy, joyful, soulful, loving, beautiful, adventurous, and meaningful moments each day.
- Balance, peace, and joy are something I strive for in my life. I am appreciative of the many blessings I receive to ease my suffering.
- Life flows through me, and I remain firmly grounded yet flexible and light.
- I am open to a new infusion of positive energy, love, and peace in my life.
- I am radiant in my imperfection. Confident in my soul. Loving in my openness. Free to be me.
- I celebrate my survival of loss with compassion, commitment, and gratitude.

To My Daughters in Heaven: Thank You

Walking this grief journey with you has inspired me to become:

- Emotionally centered.
- Soulfully resilient.
- Calm in the midst of chaos.
- Resistant to holding grudges.
- Understanding and forgiving.
- Creatively inspired to write.
- Kind and compassionate.
- Able to speak my truth.
- Heartfelt, patient, and loving.
- Aware of my value and purpose.
- Tuned into the wisdom of the afterlife.
- Passionate to share our journey.

Closing Thoughts

Thank you for purchasing my book, *Hi Mom, It's Me: Hope, Love, and the Afterlife*. It was written for you with soulful intention and heartfelt compassion to share my experiences of transforming grief beyond child loss with the hope of uplifting, comforting, and supporting you.

If you enjoyed reading it, I would love for you to subscribe to our free newsletter, Soulful Adventuring in the Mystical, Magical, and Mindful, on my website, follow along on social media: @TheArtofSoulfulInspiredLiving, join our Facebook group: Hope, Love and the Afterlife, and to share about this book with your friends and family. I would also greatly appreciate it if you would leave a review of your reading experience on Amazon and Goodreads. This will assist me in future writing endeavors and in getting this book into the hands of those who could benefit from reading it. Your kindness is appreciated with love and blessings.

For Resources on Grief Recovery, Life Saving Narcan, and more, visit our website: www.nancyyuskaitis.com

The following are the ways I have changed in the writing of this book. I could not have survived the grief journey in the way I have without the passion, persistence, and promise of my continuing relationship with my two daughters, the Soulful Starlights.

15 WAYS I'VE CHANGED BEYOND CHILD LOSS

1. I AM EMPATHIC: The depth of my empathy for others has increased tenfold with each passing year.
2. I AM WISER: The ability to tune into my soul and the spirit world has provided guidance in every area of my life.
3. I AM PEACEFUL: The awareness I possess that I am not alone, that there are beings of light, including my loved ones, working on my behalf, is very comforting.
4. I AM COURAGEOUS: The strength I hold within my soul to be a survivor with a mission of resilience, reclaimed joy, respect, and gratitude carries me forward in my desire to light the way for others.
5. I AM JOYFUL: The intention I place on observing uplifting experiences through soulful, inspired adventures is a healing path to reclaiming joy.
6. I AM SOULFUL: Connecting with my soul and the spirit world by going within, listening, and implementing healing practices has provided gifts beyond measure.
7. I AM INTUITIVE: The value of believing there is more to this life than meets the eye has developed my spiritual ability and desire to share messages from spirit.
8. I AM CREATIVE: The sun-drenched shades of color that infuse my artistic soul have woven their way throughout every area of my life.

9. I AM COMPASSIONATE: The love in my heart overflows with a nurturing vibe, offering comfort, support, and encouragement to beautiful souls.
10. I AM ACTIVE: The pursuit of wellness is an ongoing practice that fuels my soul for healthy living.
11. I AM PASSIONATE: The desire to love and share an uplifted life beyond loss is a personal mission of mine.
12. I AM GRATEFUL: The mere act of being thankful for all the assistance and blessings in my life generates an abundance of positivity that permeates through my being.
13. I AM RESILIENT: The grief encompassed my life, yet through grace, intention, prayer, and soulful-inspired adventures, I continued to re-merge with renewed purpose and passion.
14. I AM ADVENTUROUS: In body, mind, and spirit, the call to experience a variety of environments, cuisines, and lifestyles has fueled my passion for living a colorful life.
15. I AM MINDFUL: Being present at the moment and having emotional availability allows my soul to observe the natural beauty in my world and to share it with others in my life.

—Nancy Yuskaitis

Acknowledgment

Thank you to my husband, Bob, the love of my life, who has offered endless encouragement, compassion, and joy throughout all the chapters of our lives for the last three decades. Our love story is a true blessing and a continuing adventure.

Thank you to my wonderful son, who, with his beautiful family, lights up my life, and to our blended family and friends for sharing this life with us.

Unlimited thanks to the spirit world and to my team in the afterlife, especially the Jovials, who played an immense role in my writing journey, culminating in this book. The physical healing, emotional resilience, and book coaching you've provided have been life-enhancing.

My immense gratitude to the Soulful Starlights, my two beaming bright lights, my daughters in the afterlife, for the exquisite compassion, lightening my sorrow, and guiding the path to soulful living. This book would not exist without your strong desire to share your stories, offering hope and healing to those who have experienced loss.

I would like to thank the incomparable psychic medium, James Van Praagh, for his encouragement to write this story about my two daughters in spirit, who took my hand and guided my journey from a dark and tragic world into a light-filled, adventurous one. His school of

Mystical Arts provided support in my studies in Writing from Within, and becoming certified in Advanced Mediumship and Spiritual Life Coaching, which have resonated with my soul and helped me in the early stages of writing this book.

I also extend my abundant gratitude to my psychic soul family, the JOYS: Bunny Sutherland, Jonathon Hope, Naila Hope, Eve Simmons, and Susan Schmitt Arenkill, whom I met through the James Van Praagh School of Mystical Arts in 2019. Along with this circle of exquisite mediums from around the globe, we continue to meet weekly to explore psychic development, healing, and support one another in fulfilling our purpose through transformational work that impacts lives in countless ways. Your love and encouragement in every aspect of my life, as well as this writing endeavor, have been instrumental as my life transformed into a soulful grief journey. I'm so blessed to have you in my life.

Thank you to Global Book Publishing for your guidance and support in bringing this book out into the world. Your kind and thoughtful expertise is appreciated.

About the Author

Nancy Yuskaitis is a psychic medium, spiritual life coach, Reiki master, and creativity coach who channels healing through writing, art, and soulful connections. A wife, mother, and grandmother with two of her three children in the afterlife, she shares messages of hope, love, and resilience in her book, *Hi Mom, It's Me*—a true story of healing following the sudden and unexpected loss of each of her daughters four decades apart. Nancy resides in Florida and New Mexico with her husband and dog and finds joy in soulful inspired adventures, family time, and travel.

As a certified spiritual medium, her belief in afterlife communication provides hope and reassurance that life and love extend beyond our physical bodies and that our souls remain connected through time and space.

As a writer, she takes you on a journey that unfolds in beautiful and heartfelt detail, inspired by her own experiences of surviving devastating loss and rebuilding a fulfilling life while striving to inspire others to create their personal grief journey.

As a spiritual life coach and Reiki master, she brings mindfulness and meditation practices to the page for releasing grief and learning to live alongside loss in gentle, nurturing ways.

As an art therapy and happiness coach, her love of sun-drenched color, graphic design, and photography, along with original quotes, offers inspiration and guidance drawn from her life experiences and the world beyond. She understands the value of self-expression in art and journaling as a means to foster healing and reclaim joy.

Connect with the author at:

- Page: TheArtofSoulfulInspiredLiving
- Group: hopeloveandtheafterlife
- @theartofsoulfulinspiredliving
- hopeloveandtheafterlife@gmail.com
- www.nancyyuskaitis.com *(Sign up for my newsletter)*

Book Discussion Questions

◊ Did you have opinions about the afterlife before reading this book?

◊ What chapter or section of the book did you find inspiring?

◊ How do you feel about afterlife communication after reading the book?

◊ Have you ever observed a sign from a loved one in the spirit world?

◊ Do you ever feel the presence of your angels, guides, or loved ones in the afterlife?

◊ Do you have any experience with other books on this topic?

◊ Can you relate to any part of the book in your own life?

◊ What gives you the most solace in your grief journey?

◊ Do you feel encouraged to try any of the practices in this book?

◊ Has this book been helpful to you in reading someone else's story of loss?

Original Quotes
by Nancy Yuskaitis

"One day, she felt a spark of light peeking through the cracks in her broken heart."

"In this life, you may touch the hearts of those who never let on the significance of your presence in their life. Shine your light anyway."

"Bask in the knowing that you can impact lives and uplift souls each day that you are alive. Live like you are, fully alive. Live passionately, vividly, and consciously aware of the beautiful souls who share this life with you, seen and unseen."

"Set your sights on the direction you choose to go. Begin the journey with an open mind. Notice if the path becomes illuminated or stays unlit. Decide whether to proceed with full steam, with caution, or in another direction."

"Ride with us through the skies to see the bigger picture, that we are all given opportunities to grow, advance, and transcend our difficulties and challenges. Let peace reign and forgiveness be experienced to carry forward. May any and all wounds, resentments, anger, and hard feelings be released appropriately into the universe for healing."

"Messages of love and light are being transmitted to you through your heart chakra in waves of energy, one after the other, leaving you refreshed, renewed, and able to step forward, empowered and passionate to serve."

"It's been many months, and I have never left you. I am just on the other side of the veil. All you need to do is call out to me, and I am there with you. I still love surprising you with unexpected moments, and I feel great joy to hear your laughter."

"I believe that living with a resilient heart in which to hold your loved ones close in spirit ensures they will always be with you."

"Remembering you is easy; the part that is so hard is going on without you. Oh, how hard it is to miss your child in heaven every minute of every day."

"Always remember, you are loved in the spirit realm. Allow that love to fill your heart until it's overflowing. Let your entire being soak in the healing energy of love."

"SOULFUL GRIEF REFLECTIONS: In her grief journey, she realized that she was being called to expand her boundaries of what she could handle because she had been tested so many times. A choice had to be made whether to stay in that place of despair or to cry it out, express it creatively, and let it go to allow a sense of heart-filled lightness to gently wash over her, leaving her more peaceful and filled with hope."

"Grief is such an isolating process where you pull in your wings and wrap them around your heart in an attempt to comfort and protect yourself from the pain."

"Sometimes, a memory comes over her that is so intense it sends her back into the grasp of sorrow once again. She lingers there, allowing the tears to fall in a healthy expression of grief."

"Loss is a great teacher. There is no getting over it, there is only learning to live with it, tucked inside your heart."

"SOULFUL REFLECTION: I realize in my heart that there are times when I need to stay in this place of sadness and grieving, but when I feel myself slipping away to a dark place, I call on all my remaining energy to regain my true self and allow it to feel uplifted again."

"AFFIRMATION: I breathe in hope and goodwill and breathe out pain and sadness."

"Feel the peace, not the fear. Feel the love and let it comfort you."

"Be gracious. Don't hold onto emotions that no longer serve you. Seek to allow peace and understanding within you."

"Soulful Grief Reflections: My soul began to feel nurtured and loved with kindness and compassion beyond compare. Hope for better days to come started showing up in my awareness. I could find peace in fleeting moments, offering respite from my overwhelming sadness. Life held promise that I could survive this devastating loss of a child, again."

"When the tears come, you know what to do. Let them out, lovingly allow them to move through you until the crying passes. Then, fill those spaces with love and light."

"I cast off the heaviness of grief and the sadness of loss and allow the light of my heart to shine."

"Embrace the love in your life. In good times and challenging ones, it can soothe your soul."

"Cherish love. When you are feeling loved, feel the fullness in your heart. Breathe in that love and let it radiate throughout your being."

"When you are feeling loved, embrace the fullness in your heart and let it expand through your being and out to the world."

"Appreciate the people in your life who listen to you as you express your life's journey."

"My spirit recognizes truth, beauty, and sincerity."

"The beauty, adventure, love, and kindness in your world help to carry you forward as you heal from loss."

"My heart recognizes the sorrow of grief with compassion, love, and empathy."

"Blessings come in unexpected ways; all you need to do is open your heart to receive them."

"Notice how tight you feel, let go of the resistance, and let the life force energy flow through you in a way you never thought possible before."

"Soulful Grief Reflection: Sometimes, a memory comes over her that is so intense it sends her back into the grasp of sorrow once again."

"Cultivating mindfulness is simply living intentionally moment to moment with conscious awareness."

"Soulful Grief Reflections: The sound of her own laughter startled her as she stood in a circle of friends, I can't believe I am laughing again, she heard herself say out loud."

"Her purpose and passion were renewed to assist others through the understanding that life goes on beyond one's passing, and heart and soul connections remain through eternity."

"When events of synchronicity happen in our own lives, it is a reminder of the mystical and magical blending that occurs between heaven and earth."

"There is such compassion for earth-bound souls from all of us here, especially from the ones who have lived a lifetime or two on the earthly plane. There is much watching and waiting in the wings to be asked for assistance from those in need."

"There is a team willing and waiting to be of guidance, assistance, or blessings bestowed on those who request divine intervention."

*"She allowed herself to be led by the hand from the darkness into the light.
As she did so, a whole new world opened to her.
In this world, she felt renewed, restored, and radiant.
It was magical."*

"Take my hand and follow me, and we will guide you from the darkness in which you are living into the light of healing and renewal."

"A Soulful Inspired Adventure is an activity or experience that can nurture your spirit, delight your senses, open your heart, uplift your soul, and broaden your perspective beyond your current life experience."

"Every day, we are given the opportunity to observe the experiences that add value to our lives and to breathe in the enjoyment that can occur when we are mindful of the desires of our hearts."

"When you have lived with loss or difficult life circumstances, as I have for many years, you learn to actively notice and be grateful for the mystical and the magical, the soulful and surreal, the simple and special once-in-a-lifetime moments of true beauty, compassion, and connection with nature, the spirit world and life, itself."

"AFFIRMATION: I give thanks that my life is uplifted by the healing energy found in nature."

"Being kind and gracious to others you meet in your journey through life will impact lives in ways you may not realize."

"Kindness acts as a healing balm, soothing and calming both the giver and the receiver."

"Cuisine Inspired Adventures are an avenue for restorative healing."

"In your journal, let your heart express your emotions on the page without critique."

"Live creatively to discover a new or renewed passion for artistic expression in your life."

"Each day is a gift, and each moment can provide uplifting healing and joy to your inner and outer world. You are loved. May your journey be graced with mystical, magical, and mindful adventures."

Made in United States
Orlando, FL
24 August 2025